MAKE IT MAKE SENSE

MAKE IT MAKE SENSE

Lucy Blakiston and Bel Hawkins

Shit You Should Care About

Published in New Zealand in 2024
by Moa Press
(an imprint of Hachette Aotearoa New Zealand Limited)
Level 2, 23 O'Connell Street, Auckland, New Zealand
www.moapress.co.nz
www.hachette.co.nz

First published in Great Britain in 2024 by Quercus

Copyright © Annabel Hawkins and SYSCA Media Ltd 2024

The moral right of Lucy Blakiston and Annabel Hawkins to be identified as the authors of this work has been asserted in accordance with the *Copyright, Designs and Patents Act 1988*.

All rights reserved. No part of this publication may be reproduced, stored in a retrieval system, or transmitted in any form or by any means, electronic, mechanical, photocopying, recording, or otherwise, without the prior permission of both the copyright owner and the above publisher of this book.

A catalogue record for this book is available from the National Library of New Zealand.

ISBN: 978 1 86971 828 2 (hardback)

Cover illustration by Marcello Velho
Author photograph courtesy of Billy Baxter
Internal design by Clare Sivell
Digital production by Kirby Jones
Printed and bound in Australia by McPherson's Printing Group

The paper this book is printed on is certified against the Forest Stewardship Council® Standards. McPherson's Printing Group holds FSC® chain of custody certification SA-COC-005379. FSC® promotes environmentally responsible, socially beneficial and economically viable management of the world's forests.

This is for you.

It's also for us.

CONTENTS

PROLOGUE
How we got here

1

CHAPTER 1
How I make my money is not the way I die

11

CHAPTER 2
Why we need to go far away from where we came from

57

CHAPTER 3
On friendship

95

CHAPTER 4
The part where someone you love dies

139

CHAPTER 5
Phoenixing
161

CHAPTER 6
On falling in love (or not)
193

CHAPTER 7
Staying sane in the matrix
231

CHAPTER 8
Ugh, let me live
269

EPILOGUE
Tell me what I need to hear,
which is that everything's going to be ok
299

ACKNOWLEDGEMENTS
305

PROLOGUE

How we got here
By Lucy

International Relations lecture, Victoria University of Wellington, New Zealand, August 2018

    LUCY: so i've had an idea that i want you and liv to start with me
    as a TRIO

                                      LIV: EPIC TRIO

    LUCY: a blog called Stuff You Should Care About
    for people who don't have time to figure out the things that
    they should care about
    so we write little pieces so they don't have to go and search
    for it themselves

                                    RUBY: OMG
                                    I would LOVE

LUCY: do you think we'd be able to call it 'shit you should care about?'
like with a swear word?
coz that's edgy

                                              LIV: Yes!!

LUCY: like I'm just sitting in my lecture buzzing . . . we can write in our own styles or whatever and have to answer to NO ONE

                              LIV: This could be so cool OMG

LUCY: it's so OPEN and you can write about ANYTHING that you should care about

                                       LIV: yes i LOVE that

                           RUBY: Would actually be so cool
                                     I already have an idea
                                         When and where
                                             For meeting

LUCY: what you up to today / this arvo
/ tonight
bring notebooks
and ideas

The worst question you get asked when you're about to graduate from university isn't about how big your student loan is or whether you've got a boyfriend yet, it's 'what are you going to do next?'

If you don't have an answer, you laugh awkwardly in the way someone does when they haven't quite heard a question, and say something like, 'Oh, not sure; my job probably doesn't exist yet!'

Frightened at the prospect of a real world in which, as lecturers loved to remind us, there was no money in what I wanted to do (journalism), I genuinely didn't feel like I had answers to give. But the response to this question felt bigger than that. There was no money or certainty in *anything*, so I figured, if I wanted some sort of career in the only industry I was remotely interested in, I might as well try and do *something*. This thought process might tell you a little bit about my nature: specifically that I'm incredibly susceptible to reverse psychology, so if you tell me that something's not possible, I'll likely try to prove you wrong. So, as you do when you're a naive and overconfident 21-year-old, I set out with my best friends to build something entirely new.

Everyone loves an origin story. They want to know how the hell we went from three girls in a small town in a little pocket of the world to running one of the most prominent Gen Z media platforms around. The answer lies where all our angst does: the internet.

Then, they want to hear about success and how to get it. Are there secrets and magic formulas to recreate it? Do you ever feel like you really have it? That part is not so straightforward because the internet doesn't let young women simply have success. It makes us second-guess ourselves, always showing someone else doing something smarter. More noble. With better legs. That makes you question whether you deserve the success. Whether you want it. Whether you can handle all those faceless DMs and hot takes and competitive click-baiting.

But I'm getting ahead of myself.

Shit You Should Care About (SYSCA for short) started in that International Relations lecture in 2018, where I sent those offhand texts to my two best friends: Ruby, the eternal love of my life and the only one who can handle working in the chaos I create; and Liv, always lost in a painting, a song or a car park. The three of us had followed each other out of our small town and into the city: Wellington, in this case. There we were spending our late teens and early twenties (and an obscene amount of money) getting degrees in Media and International Relations that none of us were sure we wanted, and that no one was sure we'd use.

We went with the mantra 'Cs Get Degrees' (which none of us stuck to because we'd always been overachievers) until I found myself struggling to keep up with the unnecessarily boring reading and articles we had to get through week after week for class. Here I was, three years into a degree where I was literally studying power, social movements, and how the media affects the two, yet somehow, I felt less informed or inspired to learn about the world than ever before. Why weren't people talking in words we actually knew and used? Why did I feel stupid for not knowing phrases like 'hegemonic discourse'? Where was the colour? Where was the fun? *There must be a better way to make sense of all of this*, I thought over and over again as I lugged those textbooks up four storeys to my tutorial each week. In hindsight, it seems audacious to think the three of us would be the people who would find this 'better way.' But when you're a young woman in your twenties, sometimes audacity[1] is all you have – just one of the powerful forces that, we would go on to learn, would be constantly underestimated.

This was 2018, when Instagram was mostly used for saturated brunch photos and the crying face emoji wasn't cringe yet. Blogging was a dead or at least dying art, but we decided to start a blog anyway. SYSCA became a WordPress site where we wrote three posts a week about whatever we thought people should, as the name suggests, care about. Abortion laws in Texas, bullying culture on *The Bachelor*, how to beat procrastination – it was a mixed bag from day one. Like literally every publisher to ever exist, we quickly realised that you could write the best shit in the world (it definitely wasn't), but if it didn't have an audience, the impact was like the proverbial tree falling in the woods: no one heard it. I wouldn't consider us a 'publisher' until we'd been working on SYSCA for about three years, but I guess we always thought like one.

What we did next didn't seem groundbreaking at the time, although everyone seems to say it was, except tech gurus on stage at digital trends summits. We started repurposing our content and posting where we knew everyone was hanging out: Instagram. Maybe it was a wild idea to use a photo-sharing app for words, but SYSCA felt like a welcome disruption to the influencers peddling waist trainers and former high-school classmates sliding into our DMs with a 'Hey, hun!' and an attempt to recruit us into the latest insane multi-level marketing scheme. We knew there had to be a better way of using this platform. A selfie of a bunch of A-listers wasn't going to change the world, but it could become the most-

---

[1] Audacity: The naive ambition championed particularly by young women alive with the feeling that their ideas are worth listening to.

liked tweet of all time. What if we took an ounce of this attention away from the people who'd always had it and tried to do something meaningful with it? Without realising it, we developed what we could have paid an advertising agency $100,000 for: a strategy. That December, we reached 1,000 followers. Midway through 2019, we had 20,000, and by the end of that year, we had 61,000. It took me years to appreciate that the skill of seeing a story and knowing exactly where and how it should be presented was a result of going moderately viral as a teenager with my One Direction fan account – now I thank God for all those 'wasted' hours (more on that later.)

Then 2020 hit. We were locked inside, living through a global pandemic, an insurrection in the United States and Britney being freed. We were expected to be productive and get fit and bake bread and get over our exes while simultaneously going easy on ourselves, taking baths, doing face masks and not being cynical about celebrities singing 'Imagine' down the barrel of their cameras. Everyone was desperate for information but needed it in the simplest (and least depressing) form possible, because we were all experiencing the most giant, confronting, humbling and vulnerable thing at the same time. The antidote to the hell on our screens felt like it was hiding in plain sight: what if we made the news as human as it could be? If we were all going to be posting right through this weird and fucked-up time, we might as well try and make that meaningful.

In lieu of living a normal life, I started spending all my time reading, writing, understanding, explaining and sharing what was going on in the world. We called the published content 'no bullshit daily updates' because that's exactly what they were. At the same time, Ruby decided we needed a media kit in case our platform accidentally grew big enough to become a business, so she taught herself how to write one of those. Liv designed all the content in the hours between her lectures, which she was now attending via something called Zoom. We weren't a traditional news site that could rely on revenue from banner ads, nor were we influencers who were getting paid to show their PR spoils; we didn't know what we were, just that we were doing a 24/7 job completely for free. We did it because we loved it.

As the pandemic burned on, so did the pressure on celebrities to show an awareness of the world around them. Remarkably, they started coming to us for their news: three young women in New Zealand, curating and sharing digestible takes on what to care about. (It's important for me to note here that we never strayed from our intention in those initial text messages to make our content very open. Yes, we were sharing a lot of news, but we were also sharing a healthy amount of Harry Styles and reality TV content as well – we're nothing if not human!) I'd ring the girls from my childhood bedroom freaking out that we were on Ariana Grande or Billie Eilish's Instagram story or that Madonna or Joe Rogan had just followed us. Whatever we were doing was working, and by June 2020, we'd reached a million followers. By June the year after, that number had tripled. It was more than any other news site in New Zealand, rivalling some of the largest publishers in the world.

Some people made babies during those lockdowns. We were on our bedroom floors making new media. In 2020, we launched our first podcast, 'The Shit Show', having raised the money to buy a podcast microphone by selling tote bags online. We taught ourselves how to produce and edit and record and host – skills our media lecturers weren't teaching us, at a time when social media wasn't even on the curriculum.

As our stats grew to unfathomable heights, I became more and more grateful for a decision we'd made in our very first 'meeting' at the coffee shop below my flat: that we would keep ourselves out of it as much as we could. SYSCA was not was about what we looked like or what we wore; by design, when people found us, it was because of our minds and not our faces. There's that audacity again.

Social media had a particularly terrible rebrand in 2020. Fake news engulfed people's feeds and infiltrated politics more than we thought possible. Algorithms divided us. Shadowbanning (muting social media users from sites without them knowing) was happening more frequently, but was always denied by the major platforms. It was a mess. In a bid to escape the algorithmic hell we were so embedded in, we launched our daily newsletter as something we could own. In its infancy, this daily email (which cutely became referred to as 'The Newsy') was delivered to inboxes each day to round up, unpack and connect the dots of all the things going on in the world. But The Newsy quickly took on a life of its own. We started to introduce our audience to smart and funny people we'd met along the way; people who knew a lot about something or a little about everything, people who were just as obsessed with things as us.

This is where Bel comes in. We met in the shared office SYSCA had grown into and immediately bonded over our love for words and our addictive work and pop-culture tendencies. Most days, we'd collide at the front door at 9am, coffee in hand, both having been up since 5am Zooming or pitching or working on something, as we put one dream down (writing) to chase another one (paying the bills). One Thursday afternoon in the car park outside our local pub, I asked Bel what she'd been up to, and she said something I'll never forget, with a glint in her eyes, 'I've had the most terrible time lately. But you know the best thing that came out of it? Meeting people like you. You help me come alive again. You help me phoenix.'

And so Bel joined the SYSCA universe. We turned that word, 'phoenixing', into one of her first columns (aptly named 'Bel Chimes In'), and the scope of our work grew from not only helping explain the shit people should care about externally, but also what was going on inside of them. Bel taught readers new words for things that we all felt but didn't know how to describe, explored how not to rob ourselves of joy and how to move through loneliness, and examined how our internal lives are intrinsically bound up with the way the world works around us, both online and offline. Her words started to generate a kind of reverb in our community we'd never seen before. We knew we'd hit a nerve.

So that's how we got here.

This is not a coffee-table book of memes, news infographics or social media hacks that will date the second the ink dries on the page. Cringe. It is about the world and how we make sense of being in it at a time when the internet is making us, breaking us and changing everything as we know it at such an impossible speed. It's a collage of anecdotes, essays, poems, scripts and exchanges that capture the wisdom and experience we've collected by being alive and online, curious, ambitious, broken and put back together again.

We wrote this book because social media is ephemeral, and, like our attention spans, it will wax and wane and potentially even disappear at some stage. We don't have master's degrees in literature – we'll leave the refined art of that to the experts. But at a time when everything feels like it's whooshing away in an endless scroll, we want people to be able to hold the answers (or questions) about what to do with all their big feelings in their hands. Because there's so much shit in the world, so much to make sense of, so much to be afraid of and so much to feel anxious about. We hope this becomes one small, tangible thing to touch, and read, and love and refer back to in the moments when you're not so sure. Moments when you might even need a bit of that audacity:

Auckland, New Zealand, September 2022

    BEL: Big moment. Bout to go snip ties with my romantic endeavour so I can come home and write this book.

                  LUCY: good luck and you have everything you need already in you <3

Words to live by.

CHAPTER 1

How I make my money is not the way I die

*What work is, what it can be
and what it's not.*

Is this what I'm going to have to do for the rest of my life?
By Lucy and Bel

When has it ever been normal to carry your work in your pocket? Or to be logged into 17 different platforms you have to mute each time you step out of the office for a gasp of life? Will my job be replaced by a piece of code? When did we decide it was OK for work to leak so much into everything outside of it that we can't tell where one ends and the other begins?

Is work *a* thing we do, or is it *the* thing we do? Being so privy to the realities of others' lives now has pressed us up against an existential question older generations perhaps didn't have to ask: *why should work take up so much of our lives?*

Rich coming from us, we know. From the outside, you might see two young women laughing over their laptops at a café as though they're one post away from a million-dollar deal (not the case) and having too much fun. But, as always, with work and life, there's the messy reality. And when you run a business that presents as so successful on the surface, everyone always thinks 'she has it all'. And then, on top of that – 'how does she do it?'

Short answer: obsession. Not with the 9–5s or meetings that could have been emails, but with whatever we were creating, sometimes on the side from our day jobs. Up late. Up early. Lit by the blue light from our phones and screens, writing and making and believing something would come from all this extra time and effort that no one could see. For a long time, the work we loved doing started after the hours of the work we *had* to be doing. And then, when what we loved collided with how we made a living, we were faced with a new type of danger. Because, like the internet, this work has no end. It's limitless in its possibilities and the ways it can consume you. And it's so easy to let it.

We both entered the media during the exact period when news feeds were no longer run by formal media institutions; anyone with a computer could suddenly become a 'creator', watched by thousands from their bedroom floors, and anyone with a keyboard could write, armed with self-proclaimed expertise on the most nuanced and political subjects. We landed (or, in Lucy's case, created) jobs we couldn't explain to our parents (or, let's be honest, sometimes even to ourselves) using apps that didn't exist when we were studying the industry we now work in, and started producing content that reached more people than New Zealand's largest news broadcaster. There were no rules for any of this, only the ones we set ourselves. Because work is one of the few things there are no dupes for – there's no cheap alternative. No easy way out. But, dear God, there has to be a way through.

I owe it all to One Direction
By Lucy

The final night of the Oceania leg of One Direction's 'Up All Night' tour, 22 April 2012, a random bar in Wellington, New Zealand

Harry Styles and Niall Horan are less than a metre away, only a wall of glass keeping us apart. Ruby and I are trying as hard as we can to seem chill and not like the 'knicker-wetting banshees' men in the media keep calling One Direction fans, but when security guards force us to part with our life-size cutouts of the boys' faces, I sense that chill is the last thing we're coming across as. The boys are both waving, and I hope they notice our meticulously selected concert outfits, hand-picked with the legitimate hope that one of the band might spot us from the stage and invite us back to the hotel that we'd been shrieking outside mere hours earlier. We're trying to seem 25, but the fact that we're shivering outside a bar in Wellington at 1am; not old enough to drink anything stronger than a shandy, even if we were invited inside, is an embarrassing reminder that we're only 15. As is the presence of Ruby's mum, who's standing a few feet away, chaperoning the whole encounter.

The rest of the band is up at the bar getting drinks, except Zayn, who's noticeably missing, but that's okay because he's neither of our faves. Harry waves his flashlight over us and, as he turns around to join his friends, I stress about how the videos on my iPod Touch are never going to do justice to this interaction. After an hour or so, we have to leave to make our early-morning ferry back, and we reluctantly depart. On the journey home, I comb through my grainy footage, upload it to my social media accounts, type up the interaction in the way I think will get the most notes on Tumblr, and wonder if this will be one of those moments that go on to change a person's life. Feels that way.

We didn't end up outside that bar by chance. The moment had been years in the making, after my simple crush on a British boyband spiralled out of control and onto Twitter. Sixty-thousand followers later, when One Direction was in New Zealand for the first time, someone who followed me and knew I was at the show tipped me off about where the band were heading afterwards. The Wellington incident went on to become 'famous' in a niche area of the internet, and thanks to what I learnt during that intense time of crushing, you could say I went on to become 'famous' in a niche area of the internet, too.

Young girls aren't allowed to be interested in things. If you're into pop music, you're basic. If you're into the stuff your dad used to play, you're a tryhard. If you're into makeup, you're wasting your time and money and told that 'natural girls' are hotter anyway. And if you like sports, you're a 'pick me' girl. As a way of proving to ourselves or to the hobby police that our interests are worthwhile, we feel like we have to make them productive. If reading is our hobby, we join book clubs and annotate our pages to 'get more out of it'. If we play an instrument, we wonder if we should be recording our music and uploading it somewhere in the hopes of getting our 'big break', picturing those early clips as the intro to the documentary that someone will inevitably make about us. For me, crushing was no different. A schoolyard crush has always increased my attendance in class. A work crush usually leads to a better (or at least wittier) performance at the office or a brighter smile towards a customer. A crush on a boyband? Well, that's how SYSCA came to exist.

Everything I learnt about being a person online, I learnt at the University of One Direction. I enrolled in 2010 and graduated in 2014, thanks to the five hot tutors who encouraged me to show up to class. The band were coming up at the same time social media was exploding, and they were encouraged to be everywhere, so I, the student, needed to learn how to be everywhere too. In YouTube 101, I was introduced to 'vlog'-style content by way of the chaotic video diaries the band uploaded weekly alongside their X Factor performances. My assignment was to log onto YouTube, admire, synthesise, download and then chop up the best bits of these videos to use in my other classes. In Twitter 101, I learnt what it took to make the clips go viral, as well as the function of a hashtag and how to make one trend, and in Tumblr 101, I turned those clips into GIFsets.

In Photoshop 101, I learnt how to make a 'manip' (a manipulated photo where you'd insert a picture of yourself next to your favourite band member), and in Media Literacy 101, I was tested on how well I could spot the 'real' photos from the 'manips.' Live Streaming 101 was held on Twitcam, where I'd stay up until some ungodly hour to join 7,000 other fans watching a combination of bandmates sit in their lounge doing mundane teenage boy things. Here, I mastered techniques like transcribing, screengrabbing and annotating, but most importantly, I learnt how to be the first person to upload an 'update' or an 'iconic' moment to the internet. In a fandom, timing and speed were everything.

Every time the boys were up for an award, I had bonus Community Management classes to figure out what strategy would rally people together and get the votes we needed. Timetabling across time zones, writing and sharing petitions, raising awareness for a cause we believed in – it was all there. My favourite class, Editing 101, was held on Wattpad, where I learnt what self-published work looked like, but, more importantly, that if I wanted to write something, I could just go for it. The exams for this class entailed reading the most terribly written fanfiction known to fankind, and editing the grammar as I went.

I graduated top of my class because although the study was self-directed, it was the most passionate I'd ever been about a subject. I'd earned my degree in cross-platform crushing, but out in the real world, I may as well have majored in embarrassment and minored in shame. I'd been doing all of this in secret, for the same pride-protecting reason you keep your childhood crush close to your chest, and there was no way I was confident enough to put the years of experience I had in editing, community management, photoshopping, social media – any of it – to use in the 'real' world. I had treated crushing as a full-time job, and I was quickly realising it would never become one.

Each July, while he was in high school, my brother Nick would host his friends for sleepovers in the lounge so they could stay up all night and watch the Tour de France. They bought magazines with different riders posing on the covers and their favourite team's lycra (literally merch), and for that whole month, cycling was all we talked about. I sat through TV highlights and replays, learnt the names of all their favourite and least favourite riders, and I thought this tradition of theirs was the coolest thing ever. When Ruby and I would have our own sleepovers to watch the premiere of a new One Direction music video or when I'd order copies of a magazine from the UK so that I could have the one with Louis Tomlinson's face on it, that was juvenile, embarrassing and a waste of money. Nick started working in a bike shop as a mechanic, and I often thought about how cool it was that he could turn his hobby into a job. He'd roll into work after school and talk openly about upcoming races, dreamt of going to France to follow the Tour around one day (groupie behaviour), and it wasn't outlandish for him to imagine that he'd be able to have some sort of career in this field. When I realised that the same wouldn't be possible for me and my hobby, I deleted everything I'd built online. I left the communities I was a part of to go and do the complete opposite: I went to university and studied politics.

I went through the motions. I passed my exams, memorised facts instead of understanding them, and I was bored. All. The. Time. I felt unengaged with what was happening in the world and disconnected from the spaces where I had once felt so inspired. There was nothing that made me feel crazy or obsessive or psycho or cringe – all the things that I was supposed to be embarrassed by, but that made me thrive. I needed something new to crush on.

During my hiatus from online crushing, the mood online was shifting. From being cringe to crush, it was now cool to crush, and being a fan became an important tool for social change. Back when I was obsessed with One Direction, my activism didn't stretch far beyond getting justice for Louis' solo in 'Over Again', but now online communities were sabotaging the rallies of unfavourable politicians, raising millions of dollars for causes they believed in and taking over prejudiced hashtags with homemade edits. The world, which may have always been aware of the purchasing power and cultural impact of fandoms, seemed to be starting to respect the hustle it took to create that impact. I wanted to be part of it again.

Starting SYSCA was like meeting up with my old friend, the internet. As soon as I started searching, synthesising and posting, I felt old muscles begin to re-engage, and realised they were from my years of hard crushing. There were tangible things I could do for SYSCA, like building a website or writing for the internet, but more important were my intangible skills. Like being able to tell which clip from a video would go viral, which quote would work best as a tweet, where the people we wanted to engage with were hanging out online, or how to get a group of people to care about a common idea. SYSCA was new, but my love for building community online wasn't, so from the beginning, our new platform paid homage to our fandom roots by blending the news with our latest crushes (notably, Harry Styles). This was strategic: we wanted our audience (largely young women) to feel comfortable being interested both in serious things like the news, and frivolous things like boybands. It was also fuelled a little bit by spite: I wanted to reclaim the interests that I'd once felt so ashamed of, and make a business out of them.

People had opinions about this. Of course they did; everyone has an opinion on the internet. The key is to know whose you should listen to. For example, you should not listen to the ex-manager of a 'famous' influencer who decides to DM you something like this:

> Hi girls.
> Have loved seeing your platform grow and I am loving the Harry content. We all do.
> I wanted to give a piece of advice – I've been at this for a while now and I wish someone had been so honest with me when I started out.
> The news cycle is really heavy at the moment and you're

doing a great job at reporting it, but the Harry stuff seems
a little light and fluffy in amongst it all.
Maybe you could isolate the Harry content to a 'Harry
hour' of sorts and we'll know when to expect it . . . just so the
messaging doesn't feel so disjointed? Then we can still get
involved with the 'shit we should care about'!
Something to think about as you continue to grow and influence.

This was a nice gesture from a man who didn't realise that he could simply scroll on or had never known the feeling of being a fangirl. Luckily, one thing I've never doubted is my gut instinct, so I replied:

Thanks so much! This is something we've thought about and as
much as we agree on some parts, we never want
to lose our human aspect or have any of our content
controlled by other people! Thanks so much for checking in
and if people think that because we post harry styles then all
our other news is irrelevant then I think that's on them. We don't
wanna put ourselves into any boxes! <3 <3

When our strategy worked, the years I'd felt like I'd wasted suddenly felt valuable. The skills I'd assumed only pertained to the singular experience of being a fan were suddenly being transferred over to work that people respected. The validation came through the people who started following us, including leaders in the media industry who wanted to replicate what we were doing, but mostly from the fellow fans who could see themselves and their skills in what we were building.

Ten years after we stood shivering outside that bar in Wellington,

Harry Styles' sister Gemma DM'd me and asked me to come on her podcast. I spent an appropriate amount of time freaking out over what 15-year-old Lucy would have thought (probably something cringe and of its time, like 'Jesus take the wheel!') before considering what she would have liked to hear. She would've wanted to know that spending her teenage years crushing on a boyband wouldn't turn out to be a waste of time and that she learned more practical skills during those years online than she did at university. She'd want to know that she became so un-embarrassed of her time as a fan that she made it an integral part of her business. She'd want to hear that she still loves One Direction, though these days she would never track them down at a bar in the middle of the night because she's learnt what boundaries are.

As Gemma and I were chatting, I felt a type of catharsis wash over me. None of this has ever been about having to make your crushes productive by building a business out of them or hoping that one day you'd get on a podcast with the sister of your decade-long fixation. It's about letting ourselves love and obsess deeply and seeing where we get to when we don't care what people think. Plan and organise your way to the front row of a concert and be loud about it. Relish the hours you spend at the coffee shop working on a project that no one has forced you to create. Walk through the doors of the White House because they need someone with the skills to edit a thirst trap of the president. You'll make it to these places because you were obsessed with the journey. Just make sure you put it all on your résumé.

What work is
By Bel

Work is what we have to do to stay alive.
Work is a mockumentary about getting up in the morning and filling the time until you get to sleep.
Work is necessary.
Work is where your dreams come to life, if you're lucky, and sometimes it's where they go to die.
Work is, most of the time, just what you have to do to get by.
Work is both your teenage dreams and horrors.
Work is exhausting, sometimes good, but mostly boring.
Work is how you let yourself be treated and learning what's out of your control.
Work is compromise, but it's not everything.
Work is starting to sound like someone you can't break up with.
Work is what someone in a boardroom or a café thinks is possible for you, although you have other ideas.
Work is what your parents think you do.
Work is what you tell them.
Work is what they do.
Work is the thing you do, but not everything about you.
Work is corporations with too much money trying to buy you out, but you knowing better.

Work is what you post on LinkedIn to look professional and ready to be poached.

Work is earning more or less than people you love, and money being a shadowy thing.

Work is a lifelong quest not to be eaten alive by the system, which you can master if you know this: if we don't have life outside of work, work becomes our life. There will always be more work to do.

There will always be more life to live. The task is to build a way of being where you aren't having to compromise one for the other. This is where we work it out.

Working on it
By Bel

First Proper Job,
Wellington Central, New Zealand, 2013

The handbag set down on the table costs more than my month's rent. The two women sitting opposite me are so well put together I feel like I'm looking through a designer clothing catalogue. The café is nearly empty; everything that comes out of my mouth feels like it echoes in the space.

'So, what are your weaknesses?' one of the women asks. 'Oooh, um . . . Can I think about that for a second?' I reply, because just before I left the house that morning, I'd read a blog post that said this is a good thing to say in a job interview because it shows your potential boss that you're a smart woman who thinks about things. The women glance at each other and smile. One of them writes a word down in her notebook. Hired.

The day before I start my First Proper Job, I have the shocking realisation that I've got nothing to wear. My wake-up-at-5am-and-skateboard-to-work-where-no one-cares-what-I-look-like attire is suddenly an embarrassing sign of the past. And I need the future. I call a friend who owns things like blazers and pairs of brogues, withdraw the scraps of my savings, and meet her at a department store in the city. Handbag. I need a handbag and a shirt that, together, effortlessly say, 'Oh, this?' as though I grew up around casual money and know how to pair wine with lunch. I buy the four items that I hate the least from the sale rack, which remind me of an office scene I acted in for a high-school drama exam. Children acting as adults acting as workers. I'm now working in *the media*. Although I can't tell my parents exactly what I'll be doing, because I have no idea myself.

My first official salary is $35,000 (it's 2013, and rent is still less than 50 per cent of people's take home pay, but, even then, it was low), and anything that's not spent goes towards more outfits to look more like a *woman in the media*. I buy heels. Crisp shirts. I have my own stack of business cards that sit in a little container on the corner of my desk like a real estate agent. All these tiny details are magnificent justifiers of having spent $42,000 on a university degree, because I've now crossed the threshold of what it means to be a woman in the world, AND I have a corporate phone account. I am Sheryl Sandberging. I am leaning the fuck in.

And so it goes like this: waking up every morning at 6:30am, packing a Tupperware container of overcooked rice and chickpeas into my handbag and walking down the hill to the office. Clip clop, clip clop, I love the way my new high heels sound. Like I'm important and going somewhere and I've left all that early twenties angst behind. I learn to send emails (use paragraphs, avoid 'e-meet you', don't use too many exclamation marks so you don't come across as young and ridiculous), sit in on meetings, join round tables, write notes from blue-sky thinking, open spreadsheets, close deals, listen to people who've been at the table longer than me so I can have an opinion they want to agree with, and come up with ideas that will help win them awards and new business. Everything is important and everything is a big deal and the pressure and self-importance is thrilling. I experiment with lipstick (bright red or, at one stage, regrettably, dark purple) and gel manicures to feel 'finished' and I begin to associate the sound of an email whooshing off at 10pm with fufilment ('Sorry for the late reply! Crazy day!').

I don't think it could possibly get any more glamorous, but it does. I get flown in a helicopter to look at a newly built billboard, to get the real 'consumer experience'. I stay in expensive hotels, sitting in their lobbies till 3am finishing documents before catching red-eye flights to big meetings in other cities. Famous, smart people do their famous, smart advertising thing, and I watch and try to mimic what they do in my own small ways. I've never felt so important in my life, helping big brands buy television advertising slots no one my age would see, banner ads no one in my world would click on and social media space that's just been invented. I'm so new to the whole concept of what work is, work gives me a purpose and a personality.

The other thrilling novelty about being a *woman in the media* was that people were always trying to get your attention or give you things for free. Once, a famous radio station dropped by our office to give us free stacks of CDs for Christmas before realising that no one had the means to even play them. Another time, a man came to sell me space on a news site for ads disguised as journalism ('Looks just the same! No one even notices! Or cares!') and called me a 'femme fatale' because of my lipstick on the way out. Once, someone tried to poach me with a salary so low the man in charge rang me, just to check he wouldn't see me 'pumping petrol on the weekend just to stay afloat'. These are my first encounters with the shadowy, unregulated sides of work and even though there are many bright, shiny experiences of becoming a woman who knows what she's doing at work, these moments never leave me.

Being new in an industry is such a vulnerable, intoxicating time, and all I want to do is rush past it to a point of confidence where I will be worth more and never be wrong. Someone tags me on LinkedIn, and I feel famous. I win an award, get drunk and happy and tired, which seems to be the point of it all. One night, my boss and I are in the office late, working on a pitch. These are strangely happy, fulfilling times, because home is damp and where dinner has to be made, and work is where it feels like *life is being made*. My boss is the first man in my career who's interested in my ideas and he teaches me a way of seeing the world that will go on to shape my life. That night, as we shut our laptops and turn out the lights, he says, 'Be careful – if this work fills you, it will consume you.'

It's past 9pm by the time I get back to my flat, where I live with two friends and no hallway. One of my roomates has just got engaged, and another's trying to make it as a stand-up comedian. Both their lights are out. My neutral-toned Maybelline eyeshadow palette still sits on the bathroom vanity with its mouth open. The dehumidifier chugs away and I stand over it, eating two-minute noodles out of a silver bowl, the sound of the fork hitting the metal keeping me company as I eat. While I eat, I scroll, getting served up posts about people's '5–9s after their 9–5s' or motivational illustrations with captions like, 'When they're sleeping, wake up and chase your dreams.' Who is they? Why is work a chase? This must be what people mean when they talk about trying to make it to The Top.

Everything you need to know about work you can learn from *Grey's Anatomy*
South Yarra, Melbourne, Australia, 2017

A new junior joins my department (which currently consists of one person: me) in an advertising agency. Even though I'm technically a junior in life, I feel much older inside. Influencers have just been invented and the media landscape is changing so fast that if you're not online all the time, you'll turn obsolete, like a coin when everyone's using tap and pay, or an iPhone that's out of date.

I need to feel alive. I need to feel relevant. I need to justify convincing management to hire someone for my team to help me after asking for support to cut down my 70-hour work weeks. I need another cup of coffee. Junior interrupts my thoughts. He's wearing a cap backwards unironically, and now I'm wondering if I'm ageing out of fashion, too. He's asking if I can take a look at his work, which is piling up and freaking him out. He's sweet and worried and says, 'I'm so stressed about this deadline, I think I'm going to spew on the street.'

'Welcome to work,' I say warmly and know I'll borrow his 'spewing on the street' line to describe the stress of the industry for the rest of my life.

I like him, and I don't want anything bad to happen to him, and I want him to like me in some sort of industry-saviour complex. Even though this isn't something I can control, and he will one day have his own 11pm distress calls about pixels being wrong in an image to respond to, I try my best anyway.

'OK,' I say, rolling an ergonomic chair over to his computer. 'There's this scene very early on in *Grey's Anatomy* . . .'

'Are you serious?' he asks.

'Yes, and it's very important you understand it.'

I set my coffee cup down next to his monitor. He lifts his hat and combs his hair back before putting it back on, picking up his phone to take notes. 'OK, so, the doctors are new; it's like, their second week on the job, and a patient dies in the Emergency Room. The junior doctors go to declare him dead, but their supervisor comes into the room and is like, "He's not dead yet – you need to try to resuscitate him." The doctors are all like, "What, no, he's definitely dead. Look, no pulse, not a single beat." And she's like, "Nope, not dead, you need to keep trying." The day goes on, and the doctors go through all the different ways you can possibly try and resuscitate someone to the point where it gets almost ridiculous. They grow tired, really tired, and nearly give up on the whole thing; the man is clearly dead and has been for a long time. Finally, the evening comes, and after hours of heart jolts and machines and procedures, their supervisor comes back in and says, "OK, now we can say he's officially dead." The junior doctors are super confused about why they've spent the whole day trying to make a dead man come alive again, and are all like, "But, why?" And she says, "Now, you can go and tell his family that he's passed away. And you can look them in the eyes and tell them you did everything you could."'

Junior is silent for a moment while he takes it all in. 'Holy shit,' he finally says. 'That's a very good metaphor.' I sit back in my chair and take a sip of my coffee. 'But I have to ask: are you comparing working with dying?'

Take a chance on me
Morningside, Auckland, 2022

So often in work, all you need is someone to roll the dice on you. You can send your emails, build your résumé, go to morning networking events sponsored by oat milk brands, but there's a bridge between what you know you're capable of and what someone will believe. It's a feeling like: *someone just let me in the room to prove I'm good and real.*

Between all the hours of working and learning and wondering whether you're good enough, there is chance. And there is luck.

I'd been keeping a spreadsheet of writing rejections from magazines and websites for years, receiving the emails, filing them away and putting reminders in my calendar for the next socially acceptable time to send them something else and humiliate myself all over again. Such is the story of working in creative fields, and the struggle is not new, but it has intensified. The world of writing had changed over the course of my twenties; now not only did you need to be good at what you did, but you had to have a following to prove it. Random 'It Girls' were rising out of New York for having style and a point of view. If you worked in social media for a brand, you were now expected to be fluent in five platforms, filming, editing, and even being the face of content day in, day out. Magazines were publishing writers with their @ next to the author byline, followed by however many thousand followers they had. Every generation has a yearning for an earlier, more analogue experience of the world, but this was something else. The effect of being so extremely online was changing everything.

Not only did you have to prove you hadn't been left behind by the opportunities the online economy had opened up, but you had to be willing to commodify your life in order to make content that strangers wanted to see and comment on and promote in turn, their engagement acting like an insurance policy for any publisher taking a chance on you. I loved the internet but I never wanted to open up my whole life to ridicule in order to succeed. After working on an 'influencer shoot' one afternoon and seeing behind-the-scenes of its reality TV, I made three promises to myself to help me stay sane in my own use of the internet:

1) To never use it to lie about my reality (posting 'Gorge weekend!' when actually in bed with a migraine).
2) To never use it for attention or validation when I felt lonely (uploading thirst traps when feeling hormonal and bleak).
3) To never give away all the intimate details of my life (stalking should take time, effort and an above-average level of skill).

And so I kept quietly working in my side hours, putting lines out into the water, hoping for a bite. Hoping an email would change my life. And then something completely unpredictable happened: a chance came to me in real life.

One Thursday afternoon at a pub lunch with my workmates, we were sat enjoying the sun. I had a good new job, where no one asked me to 'dress edgier' for a meeting with a bank or take their coffee orders as the only woman in the room, and I was thinking, maybe this is it, maybe this is what work is meant to be. I could just about write an inspirational post on work-life balance right now. I could put this revelation on a five-slide PDF and present it to a panel on International Women's Day. Lucy, the girl I keep running into in front of the office each morning, is there with us, too. The further into the syrupy jug of cider we get, the more people have left the table for their lives outside of work, but we can't seem to leave. Her phone's lighting up every two seconds,

Harry Styles-stickered laptop wedged in between her tote bag and the leg of a bar leaner. We can't stop laughing about something that's gone viral on Instagram that day. I'm newly single and cynical, and it's about tropes heterosexual couples post about themselves online:

'Matching monogrammed bathrobes.'

'His and hers toothbrushes.'

'Man caves.'

The exchanges come effortlessly, at pace, one after the other.

'Weekend away with this one.'

'Husband creche signs outside women's clothing stores.'

'Posts with guys lined up on a golf course that say "Saturdays are for the boys".'

'Permission slips from my missus.'

'Helping with housework so you can get lucky is called choreplay.'

By this stage, I'm laughing so much at our shared disdain for online tropes that my body is shaking. Everyone is free to have their own harmless form of self-expression and to post about their lives however they like. But when you work online almost every hour of your waking life, you get a feeling not everyone can understand and so when you meet someone who does, it's a cosmic kind of collision. You both have a specific set of eyes that watch things pick up and people try to ride internet waves so quickly it's hard not to live in a semi-permanent state of jaded social commentary. It's that parallel feeling of being at a party, and wanting to both be with the fun people dancing in the living room and in the kitchen watching them at the same time.

We're still laughing. Lucy tips the last of the jug into her glass, her phone going off, the internet always beckoning. 'You should write this down and send it to me,' she says, her beaded bracelets clinking, crimped pink hair catching the light. Those ten words go on to change what I know work can be.

Women in business

LUCY: ok I've been thinking
about how crazy it is that your talent is WASTED on
copywriting
like i know it pays the bills but why is no one publishing you??
what is wrong with this world!!!
i want to publish you ♡

                      BEL: Stop. You're going to make me vain
                                      But seriously?
                                                I mean
                                I would obviously LOVE that
                            Also being published is v difficult
            And I'm pretty sure they only accept work from women with
                                          famous bylines
                  And . . . some kind of it girl internet presence
                                    and honours degrees

LUCY: nooooo
i'm obsessed with what you wrote in the newsy last week
about phoenixing
(and so were the rest of the SYSCAhood)
i just feel like . . . we could be onto something

BEL: REALLY
Um, cute
I would j'adore
Obviously
I could do it weekly if you wanted?

LUCY: um i would LOVE that
let's have a meeting before work one morning this week to discuss

BEL: i'm going to put it in your calendar under the guise of 'phoenixing'

PITCH PREP

FADE IN:

INT. MEETING ROOM — A COMPANY WITH AN EDGY NAME THAT'S EITHER A NOUN OR AN ADJECTIVE — NIGHT.

We open on a boardroom of a trendy advertising agency. Men gather, mostly all wearing black t-shirts under blazers and statement sneakers. One woman (WORKING WOMAN), early twenties in a jumpsuit and sneakers is present, typing at a laptop surrounded by print-outs covered in handwritten notes. A drinks trolley nurses cut-glass tumblers. A cardboard deer-head is mounted on the wall, next to a neon sign that reads 'make dope shit' in loopy handwriting, casting yellow light. It's late. Everyone's starting to pack up.

                  BOSS MAN
             (enthusiastically)
    So, the pitch is at 9 tomorrow. I know
    we've all been pulling a few late nights.
    But let me just say, this work is fucking

dope! It's real story *doing*, you know, not story*telling.*

OTHER WORKING MEN slung back on their chairs, sipping the last of their beer, laugh and say things like, 'Shit, yeah!' and start packing up their laptops. We see the messy boardroom table covered in takeout boxes, empty beer bottles and sheets of paper with diagrams scribbled across them in bold pen.

                    WORKING WOMAN (inner dialogue)
I'm so tired, I feel like a melted candle. I literally feel dead inside. Last night I got home from work so late that all I could muster for dinner was a quarter of a cucumber on my bedroom floor while watching hip-hop dance videos on YouTube. I wish I had washed my hair this morning. I forgot to text my friend for their birthday today. How can I be asleep as fast as humanly possible?

                            BOSS MAN
                    (speaking to WORKING WOMAN
                      but not looking at her)
So, if you could proofread the deck tonight and print out twelve copies - not double-sided - that'd be sick. I think they're really gonna go for this one.

BOSS MAN puts his Moleskine journal in his leather bag and takes out his Tesla keys.

>   BOSS MAN (CONT'D)
>   Actually . . . Do you think we should get
>   them bound? We should, hey? Bound says,
>   like, 'We've got our shit together', hey?
>   Oh, and you're all good to organise Ubers
>   for us to get there in the morning, yeah?
>   It's across town . . . we should get there
>   for 8:30, grab a quick coffee and do a final
>   run-through.

WORKING WOMAN is now standing, entering a dissociative state.

>   WORKING WOMAN
>   Um, it's 10:45pm.

BOSS MAN's phone rings. He puts his hand and mouths 'SORRY,' over-exaggerating his grimace.

>   BOSS MAN
>   Gigi babe! No, leaving now. Did you manage
>   to get a table?

WORKING WOMAN looks around the room and notices all the other men have pulled on their bomber jackets and are in the process of leaving.

Intercut scenes of Andy Sachs in *Devil Wears Prada*.

BOSS MAN puts his hand to his phone and speaks directly to WORKING WOMAN, who is by now the only other person left. He himself is halfway out the door.

> BOSS MAN (CONT'D)
> Hey — quickly, before I go — could you make sure you dress quite edgy tomorrow? Like, really cool. Like, not what you're wearing right now, something that gives off our vibe more? Speaks to our brand, you know! Maybe ask your housemate?
> (Talking back into his phone)
> No, no — I'm coming! Be there in ten. Negroni, babe, you know it ha ha ha.

> WORKING WOMAN
> Twenty grand.

> BOSS MAN
> Huh?

> WORKING WOMAN
> I said, twenty grand.

> BOSS MAN
> Babe, it's just a proposed budget in that presentation — the client won't even notice tomorrow.

                        WORKING WOMAN
            No — I will do all of this if you pay me
            what Glassdoor says I'm worth, and I will
            only do it within working hours. For an
            extra twenty thousand dollars.

WORKING WOMAN sets the stack of documents on the
table, folds her arms across her chest in the power
stance she read about on the internet and looks BOSS
MAN straight in the eyes.

END.

On being a Girlboss, a SHE-EO and making Herstory
By Lucy

It's 2015 and I'm 17 years old. 'Hotline Bling' is the biggest song in the world and everyone is trying to decide whether Taylor Swift's girl squad is feminist or not. I open up my laptop and squint at my desktop background, which tells me to 'act like a lady, think like a boss'. I glance at the clock. It says I have the same 24 hours in a day as Beyoncé.

The countdown's on. My 24 hours begin with me reminding myself that good things come to those who hustle. I'm working until my bank account looks like a phone number (I deliver the local newspaper). But first: school. With coffee in one hand and confidence in the other, I'm met with my first challenge of the day: I can't drive yet. Hmm: what would Beyoncé do?

Guess I'll beckon my personal driver (Dad) to drop me off at my all-girls school, where I don't throw punches; I roll with them. After all, queens don't do drama; they do business. Six hours fly by because I'm focusing on me until the focus is on me. I raise my hand in every class because I read on Tumblr that quiet girls don't get the corner office. At lunch, none of us waste time talking about boys. Single? No. Taken? No. Building my empire? Yes.

After school, it's time for netball practice where I'm gaining the strength I need to smash the glass ceiling AND the patriarchy. Sorry for being ambitious! Lol, jk. A wise girl knows her limits, a smart girl knows she has none.

A new driver picks me up. She's a girl this time (who runs the world?) who looks a bit like my mum. When we get home, my certified multi-hyphenate mother-driver suggests I take it easy for a bit: I'm 'running myself ragged'. They just hate to see a Girlboss winning, I tell myself. How dare anyone make me feel inferior without my consent!

By 9pm I no longer have good vibes only. I'm exhausted and Beyoncé just won a Grammy. I turn in for the night ready to try again tomorrow.

It's the 2020s now. Drake's latest album flopped. People are still trying to decide whether Taylor Swift is a feminist or not, but she's a billionaire now, so who cares? The Girlbosses I used to look up to have fallen, but we all stopped using that term earnestly like five years ago anyway.

I walk into my shared office space as a business owner (I guess), and someone makes a joke that I'm a 'bonafide SHE-EO'[2]. I want to yell 'IT'S NOT WHAT IT LOOKS LIKE.'

Here's what it looks like. The designer outfits I saw the Girlbosses wearing are my thrift store finds. The 'team' they had around them to look after the hard bits are a handful of my best friends, and none of us really know what we're doing, but that's what makes it so fun. The 5am starts aren't for meditation or Pilates, they're

---

2 SHE-EOing (used in jest): The simple experience of being a working woman, with a silent nod to the glass ceiling and gender pay gap without having to explain it. Note: you do not have to be a CEO to be a SHE-EO.

fuelled by my anxiety about what people online might be mad at me about that day. That, or I'm up because I'm just so excited to talk to all my internet friends on the other end of the newsletter. My 'lavish lifestyle' is a house I rent with my three flatmates, our recycling bin still stacked like Jenga blocks in the corner.

It looks like having to constantly explain why I don't want to 'scale up' (getting investment, hiring a bunch of staff) because I'd rather be happy than rolling in it. The 'high profile' I thought I needed in order to 'leverage my personal brand' wasn't real, because, to most people, I'm anonymous. The panels I thought I would need cue cards and PowerPoints and LinkedIn-esque headshots to be on actually only require life experience, honesty and good chat.

I've been in boardrooms where I'm the youngest person there, the only one wearing pink, and I can see in people's eyes that they think I've gotten lost on my way somewhere else. I've been surrounded by execs from Airbnb and Patagonia and other C-suite people with titles like CEO and Chief People Officer, as I introduce myself as the founder of a media company with a swear word in its name. I've been on stage in New York (still in pink, still no pencil skirt), jetlagged beyond comprehension after getting off one of the *literal* longest flights in the world, explaining to people from *The New York Times* and *The Atlantic* how to 'reach the youth'.

None of this happened because of all those cringe quotes I read online, the expensive stationery that I couldn't really afford but begged Mum for, the soul-sucking routines that burned me out, the idea that I could only get to the top on my own or the 'effortless' messy bun that actually took me an hour and definitely didn't suit me. It didn't happen by me studying self-help books or manifestos written by business people in America whose parents refer to themselves as 'serial entrepreneurs.' It happened by avoiding the millennial pink offices and opting to work on bedroom floors in shared flats. By us doing unhinged things like printing out hundreds of posters and sneaking into the university campus late at night to stick them behind every toilet door we could find. By throwing enough shit at the wall that something stuck. By telling people when I didn't understand things instead of pretending that I did (and by making that the basis of our business.) By putting friendship first, always. By saying no to short-term money. By not setting long-term goals because the world is going to change anyway. By learning how to take myself out of the equation. By getting lots of advice and only listening to some of it. By realising that I'm not Beyoncé, that we all have very different 24 hours in the day, and that whole 'Girlboss' era was cringe, anyway.

You know you're burning out when you're fantasising about burning your workplace down

Sorry I'm late, I was at home trying to enjoy life, and then I remembered I had to pay for it. Did I miss much? I miss my duvet. I miss being in my body. I miss wanting things, like being in the outside world, like laughing and eating lunch from a plate, not dripping over a plastic container at my desk. I'm here because I said yes too many times, and now everyone thinks I'm talented and capable instead of human and flawed, and maybe I'm all of that, but this has accumulated like compound interest but downhill into a kind of energy debt. And now, somehow, it's Sunday, and I'm wondering whether buying this cute item on sale is the thing that'll fix my life. Add to cart, close the tab. Capitalism is bad, but this conceptual jacket might just be the thing that I need, the thing that changes everything. Speaking of need, I need to sleep immediately because I can't wake up at 5am to Wim Hof my way out of this. I have this feeling of wanting to ctrl+alt+delete my whole life and start again, except I keep waking up in the same body in the same life, and ugh, it's me who has to change it. In the women's magazine article on my tired but amazing life, once I work it all out, the interviewer will ask, 'What's your secret?' And I will say, 'Say no. Take rest. Ask for help. If you're sacrificing parts of yourself, make sure there's an end date. Go to work, and then come back to everyone in your other life, the one that loves you, the one that loves you back.'

The feminine urge to tell people that your life's work is just this tiny thing
By Lucy

Devastating to learn that I've never had an original experience. That we all listen back to our own voice notes after sending them and panic when we have to put our change back into our wallet after buying something. That I'm not the only one paying intense attention to the flight attendants' safety briefings so they think I'm the star student, or looking out the window and wondering how the hell the moon is following the car. Even more crushing to learn that among these apparently Very Common Experiences is that most of us play down our successes like they're a document we've forgotten to attach to an email.

Small town, New Zealand, 2022

I'm currently in a web of lies with my hairdresser. I was going blonde to have more fun, which meant I'd prepped myself for two things: the Google searches that come after a few hours of staring at nothing but your own reflection ('little black dots on nose', 'how to remove hair on chin'), and the inevitable surface-skimming small talk. It's always, 'How's your day?' or 'What are you doing for Christmas?' And then, inevitably, 'What do you do for work?' Which is where the web began. Rather than telling her that I've been running a successful media company for a few years now (and that we just hosted a listening party on behalf of Harry Styles himself) I choked and muttered that I was a freelance journalist. The next questions were to be expected:

'Who do you write for?'

'What do you write about?'

'Would I have read anything?'

Based on her effective follow-up questions, I'm starting to think that *she* should be a freelance journalist, and as I'm digging myself further through the lino floor by replying vaguely with more lies, I'm wondering, why the hell didn't I just tell her what my real job was? It's not that I'm not proud of what I do – I am! – but beneath that is this nagging feeling that to speak about the success I've had is like, unbecoming or cringe or something that you should save for LinkedIn where everyone pretends they want to hear about it. I know I'm probably overthinking this and that it's hard to come across as vain while I'm sat here looking like a hacked-up Barbie doll with tin foil poking out of my head in all directions, but this is where I've ended up. The hairdresser's chair is the universal humbler.

In defence of being a tryhard

There's this meme about the 'gifted child to depressed adult' pipeline that I'm obsessed with because: oh shit, it's me. It basically suggests that if you were a 'gifted' kid in school, you probably feel like you peaked too early or were suffocated by your own potential. Or, you took being told to 'stay humble' so far that it ruined you. Relatable! It feels like we're told that constantly, by teachers, by our families, by Kendrick Lamar. It's like, 'shoot for the stars and land on the moon, just keep it to yourself so the other kids don't get jealous of you!' 'Do great things, but be extremely chill about it so you don't come across like a narcissist!!' Very confusing for those of us who are natural tryhards.

When you're an adult, HR professionals will put this idea of self-policing or being ashamed of your successes in their Power-Points and call it Tall Poppy Syndrome. They'll explain it like this: imagine there's a field of poppies planted together that are all expected to grow at the same pace. It's all going fine for a while, until one day, there's one flower growing taller and quicker than the rest. An outlier. Gross! To keep the garden looking uniform, the flower that advanced too quickly gets cut down so they're all the same height again. This is Tall Poppy Syndrome: where no one flower is allowed to be exceptional in their field.

Tall Poppy Syndrome isn't just confined to the natural world; its seeds have dispersed online. You work for free for years building a community, and as soon as you get the opportunity to make some money off all that work, you'll be cut down for being a 'corporate sellout.' The person you've watched on YouTube since they were a new creator suddenly makes enough money to buy a house, and they'll be cut down because their life is no longer 'realistic.' The small business owner who went viral online gets their big break with a feature in *The New York Times*, and they will be cut down by all the comments from dudes trying to figure out whether they've declared their tax properly or not.

But of course, things grow online, too. Hate to sound like a tech-bro, but we now live in a world that feels borderless and that gives anyone the ability to build something big from somewhere small. It's how I could imagine my life outside of a 50-mile radius growing up. It was discovering LimeWire and hearing music that wasn't from the local radio's Top 40. It was reading a blog started by someone younger and braver than me, who planted a small seed that I carried into future endeavours. It didn't matter that I was tucked away in the corner of the world; the distance to a new destination was only as long as the dial-up tone.

The internet was built for the tryhards among us who choose to believe there's a whole world out there for us to conquer, no matter where we're from or how humble that place wants us to remain. Now, we just need to figure out how to bring that energy into our offline lives.

For anyone wanting to kill the part that cringes, not the part that's cringe

Cosplay the people you hate on LinkedIn

This is absolutely not a call for us all to start writing double-spaced LinkedIn broetry or to post about how we're in the hospital, but we're so #grateful to our innovative workspace for giving us a few days off to recover. What we can take from the LinkedInfluencers is their level of delusion and unwavering belief that everyone wants to hear about the life-changing conference you attended. If people online can put their job title as Chief Awesomiser, you can tell your quiz team about your promotion.

Becoming friends with jealousy will change your life

To be jealous is to be human. It's how we got someone on the moon, how Instagram stole Stories, and it basically set the premise for the entire *The Summer I Turned Pretty* franchise. We've always been made to feel like it's an ugly emotion, something we should push down or push away. But what if it's actually showing you exactly what you want? What if you interrogated why you hated that person's poem so much, only to realise it's because you wish you were brave enough to post yours? What if you could believe that the person who's taking the piss out of you actually wishes they could do what you're doing? This might just change your life.

Accept the compliment on the first go

I have a theory that it takes at least three attempts before a woman accepts a compliment. The first response is denial or downplaying: 'I know it seems like a big deal, but it's actually not – anyone could have done it!' The second response is an explanation. This is the classic, 'Oh I got this on sale!' or 'It's really old!'

And if we don't move on to self-deprecation or reciprocation, maybe on the third attempt we'll accept it. Would be cool for us to try and do that on the first try. Even cooler to be able to believe it about ourselves first.

Learn to love being underestimated

Relinquish trying to prove yourself to people who are just never gonna get it. So what if you don't spend your days thinking about 'synergy' or ending emails with a corporate sign-off that makes you feel dead inside? Pretending to be professional to prove yourself to a man in a suit will only ever drain you. Instead, let your favourite feeling in the world become walking into a room that you know you deserve to be in, and watching other people slowly realise that.

⭐ *Lucky girl syndrome is a lie; you worked hard for that*

When you've made yourself as small as you can, yet good things still happen, you convince yourself it's all by a stroke of luck. That everything you've achieved was because of the alignment of the planets on the day you were born. The only way you shatter the illusion of luck is by knowing the truth: you deserve what is happening. Sometimes, that realisation comes with time. You can also break luck's shackles by asking for validation (because you're allowed to do that). For me, it took a dude in a bar with the type of face that was only ever destined to slip my mind, telling me that my business only exists because I 'got lucky' in 2018. Whenever I think I don't deserve this, I think of him.

If all else fails, find someone who'll speak about you like they're unveiling your star on the Hollywood Walk of Fame

One night in Lisbon, sitting at a table of personalised menus, chic candle holders and almost strangers, someone asked Bel and I the dreaded question, 'What do you do for work?'

'Oh, just . . .' I start, before Bel cuts in. 'Lucy won't tell you this, but she's actually a *very* big deal . . .' she says, and details my life in a way that makes me want to transcribe it and put it directly onto my résumé. When she's finished, we exchange knowing looks across the bread basket. This act of being each other's PR managers is something we've developed to save each other from our own tryhard cringe. When it's time to switch roles, I do the same for her, leaving no stone unturned; from her time as a wedding celebrant, to her magic as a poet, to how we ended up as friends in the first place.

Worn Out Women[3] (WOW for short) can't be their own advocates all the time; we do enough. Instead, the best thing you can do is find yourself someone who will sit beside you at a random Christmas dinner and interject before you start saying you 'just' do this or 'just' do that (whether explaining your work or simply the way you live). Let them talk about your life like it's written in bold. And then offer it right back.

---

[3] Worn Out Woman: A modern woman tired of the energy required to exist in the world. See also page 56.

Being underestimated in meetings brings me true joy. Here's how you can have it too

- Wear something cute, definitely from an unrecognisable brand. Colour. Or a hairclip. Anything remotely 'girly'.
- Disarm someone superior with a compliment.
- Wait for the other person to finish talking before you start.
- Be under 5'5".
- Smile and don't say anything when other people are talking about their investment portfolios or the latest digital trading currency, even though your own shares are doing really well. They won't ask.
- Feign ignorance about someone or something you 'should know'. For example, if someone quotes Aristotle or mentions a 'seminal' book.
- Say, 'I'd love one too' if you're asked to run and get coffee and your job is not to run and get coffee, but that has somehow been assumed.
- Be quiet about your achievements when someone's bragging about getting on the beta trial for a new tech start-up, even though your side hustle is already on the same list.
- Ask, 'What's that?' when someone introduces you as 'an influ-

encer' just because you have an internet presence.
- Smile and wave and participate graciously in the conversation until it's time to leave. Then, at the end of your goodbye, effortlessly mention an insightful statistic from a recent sports match, a piece of pop culture you've been involved in, or a fact about an industry they thought you knew nothing about.
- Sign off your emails with something personally revealing.
- Revel in the moment you defy their expectations of you. Remember the look in their eyes. Their facial expression. Keep it in your back pocket for the next time this happens (it will).

Worn Out Women

Make money, but not too much of it. Wear sneakers, but only if they're clean and not as on-trend as his. Text your therapist under the desk on your lunch break while ending emails with 'no worries if not'. Cancel dinner because the meeting's going over. Apologise profusely. Pack the right bra in a bigger bag for the next morning so it fits all the 7,000 things you need to fully exist in the world. Go to a yoga class to both cleanse your mind and have an hour of your day not on your phone or answerable to anyone but your own neuroses. Get a meditation app and ask your work to expense it. Be funny and sharp, but have boundaries and go home on time. Do the thing you love on the side to remind you that there's more to life than just capitalism. Repeat this to yourself while you're being stalked by brands all day, asking you to buy a top that will change your life. Get someone to text you back. Fall in love so that you can split the cost of living. Get a pay rise. Learn to invest because you're going to live longer. Get home before it's the next morning already. Always have clean hair. Use the vitamin C serum that works best for your skin type; you should know this by now. Send a voice note to your friend from the office car park. Check in on your parents. Check your savings account. Post something to remind the world that you're smart and funny and alive. Mute your work notifications but answer the email because you can have it all, remember? You asked for that.

CHAPTER 2

Why we need to go far away from where we came from

Growing up in the corner of the world, running away and coming back again.

She's going places
By Lucy and Bel

New York, New York. Everyone is always writing about New York. The big city! So crazy! Lights and subways and people everywhere who never sleep! Ever! Or London. The Tube! Underground! So full! All the time! Soho House! That chic suburb and that big park near the palace! The Queen! The pubs! The *history*! Or LA. They write about LA, too. So romantic and warm and health-crazed and wild, riding around with boys in cars in Silver Lake and sitting in diners until 3am among all the flashing hotel signs that you've seen in movies your whole life.

They don't seem to write about the small towns with unpoetic names where no neon lights flash and where no one famous comes from. In New Zealand, there is a specific kind of *Lord-of-the-Rings*/Narnia level of isolation that's difficult to describe to someone not from there without sounding incredibly privileged about being sick of drinking from pure-water streams. Our small towns were far from night buses, big cities or anywhere you could run away to with a passport and a tote bag – they were places where you had to summon your own magic, make your own stories and believe there was something greater out there that matched what you'd dreamed of.

Wanting to leave was less about thinking we were better than where we come from and more about being intensely curious about all those places we'd watched and read and dreamed about but felt so far away from. The women we'd dream of becoming told stories of jumping out of their windows, escaping to big cities, sneaking into gigs and reporting on bands that were touring whatever chic or grunge venue they could get in to. We had an Irish pub down the road hosting young farmers' events and regional newspapers writing about our science projects.

As SYSCA exploded internationally, everyone seemed amazed that it was run by young women in a tiny corner of the globe, because that's where the All Blacks live, not where new media is invented. We were asked to speak at events, deals were put on the table, there were authors to meet, opportunities to take . . . it was all just going to cost at least $3,000 and what felt like hundreds of 5am or 11pm Zoom calls to get there. We're lucky to come from where we do, lucky to dream about leaving, and lucky to have the option to come back. But the questions about place and belonging are more universal:

Should I leave, or is here enough for me?

If I go, how do I know where to?

Where do I belong?

Now housing is so unaffordable, the idea of permanence feels like something we talk about, like outdated technology. It's forced our generation to confront a possibly perpetual state of uncertainty about where we're going to call home, what that is and how far we should go to find it.

This search is one that divides the two of us: one likes leaving, and the other loves staying, and this is how we know each of these is just as important as the other.

Running away from east to west
By Bel

Waikura Station, New Zealand, 1992

My first home was in one of the most remote places in New Zealand. My dad had a job as a shepherd on a farm at Waikura Station, near a place called Cape Runaway, which took half a day to drive out of, only to get to the main road that wound for hours to get to the nearest town. Books for Mum to build the local 'library' were left at the back door in battered cardboard boxes delivered through a chain of farmers' wives, and the doctor arrived on horse, unannounced, needing to stay for a week, maybe longer, depending on whether there were any babies being born or anyone had any serious illnesses – none of which he'd be able to know until he pulled up.

For a long time, the millennial me who came of age with access to dial-up internet and flip-top phones found it impossible to fully comprehend that level of isolation. We moved back into civilisation when I was still a baby, but that formative part of my life – where it literally started for me, always felt so alien. *What do you mean, you didn't know when they would turn up?* It wasn't until I was 17 and studying Jane Campion's *The Piano* that I began to understand. The film, made the year after I was born, follows the story of a woman arriving from Scotland, promised to marry a frontiersman in the muddy, colonial melancholy of the New Zealand bush in the 1850s. 'That's what it felt like,' Mum, who can make anything wonderful out of nothing, said, pointing to the film stills printed out on the dining table in front of me, 'Forging a whole new frontier.'

Once I understood it, this feeling of isolation never fully left me. It's a sense of never completely knowing where I've come from or where I'm meant to be; questions I've spent my life trying to find the answers to. It's so teenage when you think about it: *where am I? Who am I?* And other angsty things you write in your diary when you're trying to self-actualise your way into adulthood. But these questions have remained constant for me as I've moved around the world, like stones I keep turning over expecting something to reveal itself on the other side. In my travels, I've come to understand this existential curiosity isn't something that nags at everyone. Some people are born into that sense of knowing. I like those people. They know their place. It seems safe there, all that belonging.

But when you don't know, you feel like you're observing others' lives slot into place and waiting for that to happen in your own. These periods of isolation make chapters of my life, and then something will arrive like a wave; I'll meet someone or go somewhere. It will feel a bit like fate. Then the wave will recede, leaving a new arrangement of my life to make sense of.

The first wave came when I was 13. My brother grew suddenly very sick, and we spent two years doing everything we could to help him recover. I felt guilty for being healthy, like I'd had an unfair dose of good luck that I could never complain about. It was a lonely and confusing time during an already lonely and confusing adolescence. The curtains were drawn shut, no one would come over, my parents talked in hushed tones about the precarious future and I wanted to quietly escape out my bedroom window to a place that felt easier to be in. In the worst of it, Mum used to say, 'This will make you real, and this will make you know love, and this will make you deep.' Wisdom often comes wrapped up in shadows like that.

As I entered my twenties, this sense of isolation moved out of home with me and became purely my own. I was drawn to stories of adventurous, mysterious female characters who seemed to carry a similar curiosity about the world. I would spend hours reading about women finding their own limits, where what's been expected of them ends and what they uncovered as possible for themselves began. I'd watch films about Robyn Davidson crossing the Australian outback on camels in the 1970s. Or Cheryl Strayed hiking the Pacific Coast Highway in the 1990s. After the stick-thin, cigarette-and-pout, Kate-Moss-1990s, adventurous women who weren't preoccupied with how they looked were suddenly considered interesting in pop culture and I couldn't get enough of them. Yet in every story, the woman is always asked the same two questions: 'What are you running from?' and 'How do you know what you're doing?' In response, they smile knowingly, as if to say, 'Something's pointing me in this direction.' I could relate to that feeling. Something calling me somewhere else, I just couldn't articulate what.

I began to think the solution to isolation was connection, and given that the opposite of New Zealand was overseas, that's where I would go, and that's where I would find answers to the questions I had been grappling with. By venturing into the unknown, I was hoping I would untangle my deep-seated sense of being so far away from 'everything' (whatever that was) and figure out where I could be peacefully, authentically myself. People either ask these questions of themselves or they're never curious; we either want to open the box or never look at all.

All of this has led to an obsession with quests, which has nothing to do with growing up in the land where *Lord of the Rings*, the archetypal quest franchise, was set (pure coincidence), and everything to do with trying to find a purpose in life. Quests are really just goals with a more adventurous name, but they aren't attached to making money or amassing physical things. They're an outside expression of seeking an inside shift. Where goals need a whiteboard and a scoresheet, quests are more of a calling that often no one else can understand. They hold us accountable to our freest selves. They strip life of its complexity for a while. They demand bravery outside our everyday lives, making us give up what's comfortable to find out what's possible.

And so, in 2016 when I was 23, I quit my First Proper Job and left New Zealand. I wanted to swim deeper into the possibilities of the world and further away from the feeling that I didn't entirely fit the mould of what I should be doing where I came from. In the years of moving around the world that followed, I lived in Australia, Asia and Europe. Wherever I was or was going, I'd often find myself at an airport somewhere, passing the time by writing down ideas of what I could do next on scrap pieces of paper and tucking them into the back of my journal to return to when I needed a sense of direction. They were ideas strangers had shared, secrets locals had trusted me with or thoughts that would come to me in fever dreams while freelance writing from a hostel bunkbed in late-night humidity. When you don't have traditional markers that tie you to a sense of where you should be and what you should be doing, you start looking for signs. I took great comfort in writing things down, trusting they would resurface when I needed them to.

Years later, when I was 27 and living on my friend Lisa's couch in Amsterdam, one of these scraps of paper flew out of my bag and onto her apartment floor one morning with 'Hike across Spain' on it. I took it as a sign.

What follows is not a travel guide because that's boring and you can just go and find it on the internet.

Bunkroom, Irun, Spain, 2019

1/35

Through my bunk bed, I can see directly into the communal bathroom where a man is peeing into a urinal, wearing nothing but the bottom half of his zip-off pants, sandals and a head torch with its red light still on. I immediately think of what a girl said at a party one of the nights before I left to hike the 865 kilometres across Spain: 'I hear that hike's an absolute sex fest. Just fucking new people every night. Wild.' I want to take a photo and send it to her, but obviously that would be a gross invasion of privacy. Plus, we didn't add each other in the moment, and now too much time has passed for her to remember the joke. I make a mental note of the absurdity and guess I'll be living nomadically with this man for the next 35 days.

2/35

Everyone is obsessed with small plastic bags. Their rustle is a form of torture that will haunt me for the rest of my life – the sound of people getting up at 5am and trying to find a carabiner in an old supermarket bag. It will be played at my funeral if I don't do anything good with my life. I've accidentally brought a backpack half the recommended size and have had to become extremely good at taking up as little space as possible, squatting on the floor, rolling everything to fit. Kitty, a social worker from the Netherlands, bends down to help me zip it all in. Apparently, this ritual's called 'the squeeze', and we laugh as I commando wrestle my bag on the floor. 'A trick most women are good at without even knowing,' she says and extends her hand to pull me up.

7/35

Marous, my trail mate, is teaching me the art of foraging in convenience stores. The ritual goes like this: one of us minds the packs, while the other goes in to find an ensemble of things we can eat for under €5. She emerges with a tin of pimentos and a pack of corn thins, and we eat them straight off the tin lid, on a park bench in the middle of a roundabout. Before we heave our packs on, she pulls out a tiny notebook she's bought on one of her escapades.

'For you,' she says. I open it, and my name's been written on the inside cover in a careful cursive font. 'Make sure you write all of this down,' she says, gesturing around us. We've been joking for the last week about the motivational quotes we hear people exchange to encourage each other. It's sweet, but we're cynical. 'Plus,' she adds, 'Now you have this, you'll never be lonely.' I start to cry, either because it's so nice or because I'm so tired and have spent the last week wondering when the poetry of this quest that all the travel blogs seem to boast about will kick in. A line of schoolgirls spill out onto the pavement opposite us and laugh at us, looking like two medieval men sitting in the middle of a roundabout. Perhaps they're wondering who they'll become.

11/35

We make it to the monastery too early because everyone's chill but also secretly wants to prove they're the best at walking. While we wait for the monks to open their underground bunker for us to sleep in, they emerge with crates of craft beer.

'What's a side hustle?' Louie, a retired Catholic-school principal who's on his sixth hike of this kind, asks. Someone replies that inflation has even managed to affect monasteries and that the monks have ventured into microbrewing to stay financially afloat. I've developed bronchitis, so I take my pseudoephedrine and doze on the grass while he reads aloud from a book on Seneca. I'm quietly grinning, thinking about my inspirational quote art business.

'OK, let's examine this one,' he says, '"He who is brave is free." What do we think about that?' I drift off to sleep, but at one point, I hear him say, 'A lot of life is boring; no need to make a big deal about it,' which I store away in the back of my brain to think about forever. A few hours pass, and the philosophy continues. The gong sounds. Plastic bag shuffling time.

12/35

Profound thought: walking is the only thing that makes sense any more. Might think of something spiritual to post about this later.

13/35

Six of us spend the night sleeping in a tree hut a family has built at the bottom of their garden. They cook us dinner, do our washing, pour cider into cups and ask for absolutely nothing in return. It's a generosity I've only ever seen from people who don't seem to have a lot materially, but give what they can anyway. Once everyone's repacked again, we lie in our bunk room under the low roof, passing around someone's head torch, telling ghost stories in all our different languages. A German guy laughs so hard he nearly wets his sleeping bag. It's nothing magnificent on the surface, but I still can't believe I'm here. I pull on my eye mask. I feel ripe and safe and superior to anyone who hasn't gotten to experience this.

14/35

Meant to be having some significant epiphanies that are going to change my life forever, but all I can think about is how much I'd like to lie down for a very long time somewhere warm. Somewhere with no internet, but where I can also somehow make enough money without destroying the environment. What is that job? I want that job. I try to distract myself by listening to podcast interviews with people who failed but ultimately triumphed, despite their trying circumstances. My failure is that I want to text my unresolved horny tryst from years ago, just to see if he still occasionally gets drunk at corporate events and thinks of me. If that were true, then maybe we'll run into each other in a fatalistic way, and I'll stop self-evaluating, and everything will be complete. Will compose message after lights go out.

15/35

Ate almond Magnums on the side of the road with Kitty. Glad I didn't send the text. Turns out I was just hungry and needed someone to talk to. We haul our packs back on, complaining about the plastic bag sound. 'Don't they make fabric bags?' we wonder aloud. She's crass and kind, and it feels easy walking alongside her. I'm wondering what message she's carrying for me, and she's wondering what to do with her brother's ashes in her front zip pocket. I listen quietly. She tells me she knew he was dying before she even got the call. 'We think we have so much time, but we truly don't.'

17/35

Can only find an XXS three-pack of Hello Kitty knickers to replace my underwear that's disintegrated in the heat. In the store changing rooms, I heave off my pack and squeeze my legs into a pair before catching sight of myself in the mirror. I look like a haggard band member of Incubus after a world tour and I laugh to myself. Looking disgusting is so freeing – another inspirational quote I will write down in my tiny book. Back on the road, Marous and I veer off the track to go swimming in our new Hello Kitties. A pair of 70-year-old women are already down on the sand, peeling off their hiking gear to do the same.

'I don't know if things have ever felt this simple and good before,' Marous says, cutting an apple into quarters with her Swiss Army knife and playing 'Only You' by Steve Monite out of a tiny speaker. I stretch back over a rock, leg hair grown out, wiry pubes sprouting through my tiny underwear. My thighs, which have previously been called 'the tree trunks of New Zealand' and 'rugby player legs', flop over the rocks. It's the first time I've properly appreciated what they've done for me.

19/35

Sitting at the table, Uli pulls a note out of a small envelope, which she translates from German into English in a soothing evening ritual for anyone who hasn't heard from home but can't face the plastic bag rustling of the bunk rooms yet. There are 120 of us in one room tonight. Disgusting.

'Who wrote you these?' I ask.

'My husband,' she replies. 'He said to me, "I know if I let you do this on your own, you'll come back to me."'

'Doesn't he worry about you being so far away?' Louie asks, looking up from his iPad.

'Of course not,' she says, shaking her head. 'Besides – worrying robs us of dreaming.'

That night, in the bunk room, I get a message that my brother's ended up in the emergency ward with septicemia. Turns out we're all running away to see how far we can go before we have to turn back.

21/23

I was happy and stupid and free just two days before, and now I'm up late, worried about back home while I'm here, chasing down a quest that I thought would somehow be fun. Hiking across a whole country now seems wildly frivolous, and the contrast is hard to reconcile. I call my mum and my sister in the hospital ward, but the time zones are unforgiving and there's not enough news to update me with. I think about going home and wonder what that would achieve. My mum and sister there, trying to look after everything, and then me, also always trying, but instead, always distant. The family roles we make for each other just seem to be that way. In my dreams, I try to be in two places at once: here, in my body and real life, and over there, across the world, trying to help when I can't. Joy feels loose and easy until the string's pulled tight.

25/35

Hill. Hot. Long. Beautiful. Endless. I'm about to go back to my failure podcast when the Canadian investment banker sidles up to me. I've learned to avoid him, because he plays The Kinks' song 'Strangers' out of his phone all day on repeat. But he's so much like a character from a movie I can't help but indulge in his company.

'Yeah, I'm pretty fucking broken-hearted,' he breathes. 'You can probably tell,' extending his arms open like a bird, his walking poles dangling from his hands, yelling into the valley, 'Third divorce!' It echoes into the valley. 'Usually, I run the hell away from pain, but this time – this time, I'm walking all the way through!' And that's enough. I offer him a cashew nut before pressing on ahead. But I can't shake how much he needs this to mean, how while we walk, we leave ourselves. We're sort of . . . walking to keep falling in love with being alive. Isn't that the biggest reprieve from the chaos of modern living there is? Oh God, I'm turning evangelical.

32/35

Some of the towns are silent, as though cowboy movies were once shot here and then immediately deserted after filming. Washing blows in the wind, although there's no one around who it seems to belong to. Wild roses climb along fence lines. Dogs bark on chains. I pull into a taverna to order a drink, and hoon half a pack of biscuits like I've never had a meal before in my life.

'Memories are what cause us the most pain,' the bartender says – another one for my inspirational quote art business. It's just me in the bar, and the football playing on a TV overhead.

'Why do you think people walk in the first place?' I ask. It's obvious nothing is less exotic to him than another person in hiking gear trying to rinse the experience for meaning, but he smiles as he wipes the bar down with his swallow-tattooed hand.

'To release themselves from pains they didn't even know they had.' I get a text from Mum to say my brother's come out of hospital alive. 'I thought of you today,' she says, from a city different from where she lives, 'sitting in this place I've never been, not knowing what will come next. I don't know how you do it.'

This will make you real, and this will make you know love, and this will make you deep.

36/35

Once it's all over, I stay on at Fisterra, the lighthouse town on the coast for a couple more days, sleeping in a cheap pink hotel with soap in packets that say, 'Life is good' and lavishly starched, white sheets. Nothing needs doing, although everything has changed. I need to get back to reality and make some money in the extremely close foreseeable future. I sit in the chair at a hairdresser overlooking the sea and ask her through Google Translate to turn my yellowed hair back to blonde. She's balancing a baby on her hip, and we're laughing. It feels oddly intimate to be in the soft company of women helping each other look good again, exposing, almost like I've lost my femininity somewhere out in the wind among all the zip-off pants.

'You walk all this way, only to come back where you start,' she says, gently taking the bobby pins out of my hair.

'Where's that?' I ask. She laughs. Foreigners are always laughing at each others' decisions. Where are you from? Why are you here? How will we know when we're in the right place?

She points to the shitty offcuts of my hair on the floor.

'You.'

Running away ends where the old self stops, and the new one begins.

Music festival, Auckland Viadut, New Zealand, 2023

Homecoming

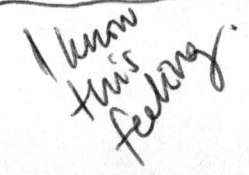

Years later, after a bad, wet summer, I'm at a music festival on a wharf back home. Things had been bad for many reasons, most specifically, that I had been home in New Zealand for three years but not 'home, home,' for half of that time. Cyclones had swallowed the roads I'd spent my teens driving around on, and going back to where I grew up was not as easy as it used to be. If you go away, you risk building a life that splits you in two: the one where you leave and the one that carries on where you left. I felt guilty for wanting a life my parents didn't get to have. It left me wanting to achieve so much with my own as compensation for everything they'd done to help me get it. We take, we push away, we try to pour back: family love is complicated like that. In the movies, home is swimming pools, and traditions, and always being together. Sometimes it's that. But sometimes it's not.

But today is about escape. Vee, Eliza, Jaz, Bre and I haven't been all together since before uni ended and we all went our separate ways. You only realise how rare frivolity and freedom are when you haven't had them for a while. We're sprawled out on a set of concrete seats in outfits we jokingly call 'Jeans and a Nice Top', watching the dancing crowd swimming in a mess of drinks and vape smoke, friends grasping each other like they hold the answers to all one another's secrets. We're older, with our own sets of keys and emails we're not answering. We know about the cost of living and that none of this can go on forever, but we may as well try. But it's more than that, though, as it always is with friends that sit in your bones. We've all come to know that a decade's worth of stories and angst and success and nemeses can't quite be replicated, because it's only our old friends who've watched us change. Amid the haze of it all, Vee turns around and looks at me with glittery eyes. We've been living around the corner from each other for over two years and I've never in my life been so emotionally dependent on and looked after by someone.

'Bel,' she slushes. The drinks are starting to hit. I feel famous, like I could make a speech in public or walk into an expensive restaurant without caring.

'What will I do without you?' I shout back. She's leaving for Kenya soon, and me for Portugal. I'm worried that this good part between us is over, and life's turning has closed down our season the way it does when friends fall in love or get job offers overseas. A guy in steampunk goggles interrupts us.

'Either of you got a cigarette?'

'What am I, a shop?' I reply, 'Sorry, but go away, we're having a moment. Go and ask that man over there.'

Vee laughs. Like, full belly laughing. And all the years of our life together spill over between us: the bottle of whisky she bought over with an oversized t-shirt when she helped repaint my apartment; the rotisserie chickens I'd pick up from the supermarket on the way home that we'd make fried rice with and malaise about in her living room eating; the parties; the hangovers; our clothes on each others' floor; the SOS calls. It's both incredibly vulnerable and overwhelming that I feel like I've become my full self in her company. 'I'm going to tell you something I don't want you to ever forget.' She grabs my hands and puts them on my temples. The music thuds in the background. My polyblend top is racing up my back, my belly popping over my skirt and my green Maybelline eyeshadow slipping down my face. I don't care. I never have to care when we're together. 'In here is your home. No one can take that away from you – ever. When I'm not with you, I'm always in here. Always.'

There's a scene in the film *Lady Bird* where Lady Bird herself, a teenage girl stuck in Sacramento, is dreaming of a life beyond her home and desperate to get as far away as possible. She yells at her parents, 'Give me a number! Give me a number of how much it cost to raise me, and I'm gonna get older and make a lot of money and write you a cheque for what I owe you.' She's young and obviously misses a point, but she also has one. We'll never fully be able to repay the emotional cost of being raised. It's an irreconcilable debt. When we're young, home is where we've come from, but when we leave, home becomes what we make of our lives. We think it's this fixed accumulation of things, but the ways we can build a home in our lives are infinite. What if it isn't bound up in this idea of a physical space filled with elegant ceramic objects and mid-century armchairs that perfectly catch the Instagram light, but something more metaphysical? It takes work to truly believe this, but it's not an impossible state to reach, where you can truly feel like, *Everything I love is here, at this moment. It's all these things I can't touch.* I've travelled so far away to find this feeling, and come to discover it's both a tangible and intangible thing.

The film ends with Lady Bird in New York, hungover after getting black-out drunk and waking up in a hospital ward. She's smudged in mascara and last night's clothes on a bright morning: when all our bad, misplaced thoughts come back to haunt us. These are the moments when we want home the most. She pulls out her phone and calls Sacremento, but no one's there to pick up. She says down the line into the answering machine for her parents to hear when they get back from work, 'I wanted to tell you, I love you . . . Thank you.' The film ends there but if it was real life, she would go on. She would go on to take chances between where she came from and who she could possibly be, who she will come back to and what she will let go of. What's that saying? *She who is brave is free.*

FUN QUIZ:
Should I escape my life, or am I just tired?

- Do I hate how I feel, or hate where I am?
- Am I sad because that's a normal experience of life, or is it something greater?
- Do I think I'm unfulfilled just because I've seen someone else's aesthetically pleasing life on the internet?
- Am I hungry?
- Lonely?
- Am I bored because I've stopped trying, or do I genuinely need newness?
- Do I really think I would thrive staying in a 10-person dorm, or should I just go camping for the weekend?
- Am I mad at my work because it's bad, or am I giving it too much of my energy?
- When was the last time I did something that made me feel alive?
- What am I not doing?
- Do I have enough experience to get a job somewhere new? Is this a ridiculous idea, or just ridiculous to someone else?
- Am I thinking about myself too much?

- Am I thinking about what someone else is thinking about too much?
- Have I had enough silence, or too much?
- Could this be solved with a mall massage and a shower cry?
- Am I giving too much because I'm afraid of giving to myself?
- When was the last time I asked for help?
- Is there a hole in my life that I'm filling with emails?
- Can I take a break from ambition to build out other areas of my life?
- If I was, say, running away, what would it be from?
- If I was, say, running towards something, what would it be?

Saying an Irish Goodbye to a whole country
By Lucy

Penha de França, Lisbon, Portugal, 2023

These are not signs from the universe. These are not signs from the universe. These are not signs from the universe. But my passport got lost in the mail somewhere, the longest of my four flights got cancelled and now both of my suitcases containing, oh – just everything I own – are missing. Cool, cool, cool. What am I even doing here?

WOWOWOW though, this is the most beautiful city I've ever seen! Can't wait to spend my first day here sweating my way through an industrial shopping mall buying unethical clothing that doesn't fit right so I can finally get out of my wine-stained plane attire.

Ouch! That feels like a bee sting. Or it could be the most deadly spider bite I've ever endured? Hmmm, better go to the emergency room.

Why are the people who work here so mean to me? Is it because I came here for a bee sting? Thank God I have Bel here shoving her phone into my hand and letting me swipe on Bumble to take my mind off everything.

Just saw the doctor. She laughed in our faces. At least I don't have a deadly spider bite, I guess.

Just had my first-ever plunge in the Atlantic. I think it's healed me. Except, for some reason, I can't stop thinking about how I don't have the right boobs to sunbathe topless. Also, why did my parents never teach me how to surf?

Cute, a text from some people I met through a few rogue Instagram DMs asking me to come out tonight. Hmmm, nice to know they want to hang out, but I might see if Bel wants to watch *Gilmore Girls* at our apartment instead.

It's raining a lot here now and I'm starting to get cold in my bed at night. Feels like too much commitment to buy a duvet though.

Baby's first Schengen trip! Am I sweating so much because I'm panicking? Or is it that the AC is broken on this plane and it's over 30°C out there? Who's to know?

Thinking about my chipped toenail polish drinking cocktails in France in what was once voted the 'Best Hotel Bar in the World.' Bel is somewhere talking to a B-list New Zealand celebrity about 'gumption' and I'm busy falling in love with an advisor to the Mayor of Lyon. Maybe I picked the wrong country to move to. Why am I dreading going back to Lisbon?

Ohhh it's because of the tax. And the visas. And the lawyers. And the accounting fees. And because I left my family. And because I can't crack a joke in Portuguese. And because maybe I don't want this?

Of course you want this. Who wouldn't want this?

Well, why can't I get out of bed then?

You know you can go home, right?

No, I can't.

Why not?

Because I made such a big deal of having all those farewells and now I'm going to have to tell everyone it didn't work out. It's EMBARRASSING.

Lucy, it's not embarrassing. You only get one life, and if things aren't working out, then the best thing to do is make a decision.

Ugh, brain, stop using my own logic against me, I'll book the flight.

You take the girl outta the regions, not the regions outta the girl

When you move to Europe without ever having seen a euro, people will call you brave. It's funny how easily you can lean into that when you're running solely on the elixir of possibility.

Here I was, chasing down the dream. I'd moved across the world to live with one of my best friends in the most beautiful city I'd ever visited, writing the book I wish I'd had as a teenager. In my head I was going to be a Euro Girl, mincing down cobblestone streets, drinking limoncello and zipping to a new country for the weekend, because (unlike in New Zealand) you can do that here for less than a week's rent.

The moment I touched down, something wasn't right. It was a familiar feeling, but one that I pushed to the back of my mind, promising myself that this time would be different. I put my discomfort down to the initial drama of lost passports and luggage and figured that once the admin was sorted, I'd feel like me again. I did all the things I thought would work. Befriended the boy at the local kiosk, frequented a chic wine bar with Bel for an after-work spritz, ate sardines in the sun, rode scooters up steep hills in the warm wind, found a group of friends and forced them to join a quiz team with me, I even started attending a writing group. This life was good, but it wasn't mine.

The more I lived in it, the more I thought about the person I used to be, who could talk to strangers, lecture to crowds, spend days on end alone and be fine with it. I was a few months in now, and it felt like all that bravery had been sucked out of me. I'd lost count of the supermarkets I'd walked in and out of without grabbing anything because I was too anxious to wait in line and talk to the shopkeeper. Cafés I'd peeked inside and decided I couldn't figure out how to ask for a table so it was easier not to go in. Phone calls I'd screened because I couldn't predict what the person on the other end was going to say.

It'd be easy to put it down to feeling unsafe in a new city, but truthfully, I felt unsafe in myself. I used to travel without fear of what could go wrong, and now I was Googling how close I was to a hospital in every new place I visited. The only times I felt safe were in the few hours at either end of the day when I'd ring my family, but somehow, even that led to me thinking about unhinged scenarios, like, what the hell would I do when they died. I wondered how normal people coped with things like this and why I couldn't.

My brain was betraying me, planning my exit strategy before I'd even arrived at the party, and no matter what I tried, I couldn't get it back on my side. It's scary when that happens.

Ruby rings me to talk about work and, in between items on the agenda, says, 'Luce, are you happy?'

When someone asks you that point blank, it feels like there is only one answer: of course I am. But I can lie to her about it as well as I can lie to myself, which is the blessing and curse of having bone friends.[4] I tell her I'm not and that, for what I think is the first time in my life, I'm feeling ashamed.

---

4 Bone friends: Friends who've known you for so long, or know you so well, it feels like they understand who you are right through to your skeleton.

In its worst moments, shame makes you feel like you've got a defect. It made me believe that I wasn't qualified to do my job, to hold down new friendships or, as I repeated in my group chat, 'do normal things' like move cities without having a breakdown. I could deal with the sunk costs of all the money, time and stress I had poured into this move. I could even deal with what I knew was going to be a hellish 40-hour journey home in my anxious state. But what I couldn't deal with was the shame of having to tell everyone I'd failed. Not just my family and friends but the audience I'd brought along for the ride. This felt like their dream, too. Shame makes you turn on yourself, makes you feel inadequate and puts all the blame back on you. Shame doesn't take into consideration that sometimes things just don't work out. Shame doesn't let you realise how brave it is to admit that.

Blenheim Airport, New Zealand, 2024

When I arrive home, I'm a mess. I've picked at my face so much during the flight that I look like a 12-year-old boy who hasn't learnt how to shave properly yet. I hug Mum, who tells me she's so glad I'm back, and Dad bundles me into his truck to take me back to the room that I'd packed up only a few months ago. Everything's the same here. The old cat I said goodbye to for what I thought would be the last time is still meowing, and the magnet on the fridge still says, 'Sarcasm is just one of the few free services we offer in this home.' The only notable difference is in me. I'm convinced the old Lucy will come back.

A week or so later, there's a trend going around on the internet with the audio, 'I think I like this little life.' Even though it's very quickly turned from an earnest gesture where people post snippets from their own 'little life' into something everyone is making fun of (such is life on the internet), I can't help but think it belongs to me. This whole experience – of having the dream but not wanting it, of having a chic life but it not feeling like yours, of feeling like an alien among all the romance of the city and then a failure for leaving it all – has shown me that a 'little life' is exactly what I want, at least for right now.

I never used to think about the concept of home very much. I assumed it would find me, or I'd be led towards it by a job I wanted to follow (or a partner, for that matter). Without the absence of outside strings pulling you in one direction or the other, home is complicated. I'm lucky because the door is always open to a family who are ready for me to walk through it whenever I need, I have friends who give me a word-for-word script to say at the doctor or who let me lie on their couch and watch reruns of *Love Island* in between therapy sessions. But I'm mostly lucky that I've got my brothers, who, more than anything, taught me that home is wherever they are.

Home is the floor that's lava and the pillow pits we dive into. It's letting me follow all the road rules on *Grand Theft Auto* without getting annoyed. It's standing on the side of the velodrome or the soccer field. It's the park where they taught me how to photograph stars. It's the lake where they live now. It's being trusted with the other PlayStation controller. It's getting 'square eyes' thanks to *Super Simpsons Saturday*. It's participating in their home movies. It's the fudge that never sets properly. It's knowing they'll always be braver than me because they can dive into sleeping bags headfirst. It's never having to set up my own tent. It's being a passenger princess on the tiny boat because they don't trust me to drive. It's speeding down dirt roads listening to The Lonely Island. It's them backing the trailer every time. It's never remembering a fight. It's only ever being punched once, and only because I deserved it. It's watching them get drunk for the first time. It's doing their homework for them. It's calling them in sick when Mum wouldn't. It's having someone to wake up early with on Christmas. It's them telling me I look pretty on my way out the door to a party. It's not falling apart when it went from Mum-and-Dad's-house to Mum's house and Dad's house. It's being separated but never being apart. It's the swell of pride when you get to say you have three of them. It's the pit of my stomach when people ask me how many I have now. It's what makes it so easy to come back; it's what makes it so hard to leave.

Home requires more than just a duvet and a visa. It's the people you love, the rooms you feel safe in, the arms you walk back into. It's building your own doors to walk back through and finding family in your bone friends when you need to. It's sacrificing what you thought you wanted for what you know you need and striding through the shame it can take to get there. Turns out, to know what might be good for us, we must first be prepared for it to be bad.

WAGS

NZ vs Italy, Parc Olympique Lyonnais, Lyon, France, 2023

LUCY: oi, phoenix
where are u

                    BEL: Waiting in line for the bathroom
                    Actually maybe it's the bar
                    Or the changing room
                    Do you think these lanyards get us into the All Blacks
                    changing rooms?
                    I feel like yes
                    Wait
                    Where are you

LUCY: no, bel I'm dying
i'm in our seats
game has begun
the woman next to me just asked if we were WAGS
and who we were married to
and I just invited myself on their family holiday

BEL: HAHAHA
Ok I didn't tell you this but
On the bus on the way out here
I asked one of the crew if they thought Dan Carter
would do us a solid
and kick a copy of our book over some rugby goal posts
as a publicity stunt once it's published

LUCY: NO YOU DID NOT

BEL: Honestly?
They seemed keen
All signs pointing to yes

LUCY: i never thought i would be here
in a lanyard
in FRANCE
being mistaken for a WAG

BEL: I know, I feel incredible
Our dads would be proud
Even though we had to google the captain this morning
Let's not tell them that part

LA DOLCE VITA

FADE IN:

INT. RESTAURANT - NIGHT

WOMAN ALONE, late twenties in a white linen dress sits at a small, red-and-white chequered table in the courtyard of a restaurant. The space gently buzzes with bronzed tourists and locals eating seafood and drinking wine. TWO MEN who could be boys shake drinks behind the bar. Strings of lights catch the bougainvillaea creeping along the stone-washed walls.

MAN IN NECKLACE, mid-50s, very tanned and fairly good-looking, dressed in an half-buttoned-down white shirt and a necklace approaches her table from the bar.

>   MAN IN NECKLACE
>   (gesturing to the tan line along her
>   collarbone and smiling)
>   Looks like you're having a beautiful
>   holiday.

                    WOMAN ALONE
               (looking up from her book)
          Thank you. I am.

                    MAN IN NECKLACE
               (pulling the chair opposite from under
                    the table and sitting down)
          Mind if I?
                         (beat)
          What's that you're reading?

WOMAN ALONE closes the book and places it face-up
on the table, revealing the cover of *Kitchen
Confidential* by Anthony Bourdain.

                    MAN IN NECKLACE
          Ahh, Bourdain. Such a tragedy he's gone
          . . . Amazing man. I actually met him
          once. On the Mekong in Hanoi in the 90s
          — that's a river. Well, a whole network
          of them, actually. That was probably
          long before you were born. Let me guess
          — 22? 25?

                    WOMAN ALONE
          27.

                    MAN IN NECKLACE
          Ahhh, but you don't look it. I noticed the

second you walked in. And all alone? Hard
to believe that.

>   WOMAN ALONE

I'm just here for myself.

The restaurant continues to buzz around them, no one noticing their exchange.

>   MAN IN NECKLACE
>   (smiling flirtatiously)

Come oonnnn — no holiday romance? It makes everything so much better.

>   WOMAN ALONE
>   (laughing gently)

Honestly, I'm having a good time. Why is that so hard to believe?

>   MAN IN NECKLACE

Sorry, I didn't mean to offend you. I just hate to see a beautiful woman eating alone. It's a travesty, no? Somewhere as beautiful as here . . . The island — it's a romantic place.

She sips slowly from her glass of wine and looks out to the street as if to summon a moped to pick her up and take her away.

                    MAN IN NECKLACE
                  (following her gaze)
            You know, I had a woman once.

                      WOMAN ALONE
                       (smiling)
            So did I.

                    MAN IN NECKLACE
            So she's a feminist!

                      WOMAN ALONE
            She's on holiday.

                    MAN IN NECKLACE
                  (shaking his head)
            You young women, you think you can do
            everything . . . you think you can *have*
            everything. Well, you can't. It just
            doesn't work like that! You think you're
            fine alone, but you're not. You *need*
            someone. We all *need* someone! We just do.

TWO TANNED FRIENDS rush into the restaurant and toss a set of apartment keys onto the table.

                    TANNED FRIEND #1
            Oh my god, sorry we're so late! We got
            locked out of our Airbnb!

                        WOMAN ALONE
                     (smiling coyly)
            You're here! Totally fine — this man was
            just telling me tonight's specials.

            END.

What not to forget

A couple of shirts for covering your sins. More swimsuits than you think you need. Something long. Something very short. One tiny thing from your old life to remember who you once were. A slutty top. A warm jumper you'll get sick of. Something you'll only wear once. Something you'll regret. New socks (old ones always feel a bit shit). A tiny card with the Blu Tack still on its corners to press into your new wall. Less than you'd think. More than you'd like. A tiny comb that folds into your hand to bring out quietly in a restaurant bathroom. A soft pant to cry in. Shoes to go dancing in. An ergonomic, nondescript outfit to walk up steep hills and yell into the wind wearing. Adaptors. Too many cords that'll never be neat. A notebook. A book you'll want to say you've read. One expensive thing to worry about losing at all times. Something to make you smell nice. One small bag and one big bag. Get rid of the rest. Leave room for the unimaginable.

CHAPTER 3

On friendship

Giving platonic love the same energy as romantic love, if not more.

Saw you out with all your friends. Looked fun
By Lucy and Bel

The internet has made us feel like friendship needs to be this Polaroid, lens flare, jump-off-the-wharf-into-the-river, 'to the moon and back' kind of experience that lives on our camera rolls and shimmers on our screens. Unless you're watching diary-entry videos of people crying into the camera about their overwhelming loneliness, it can feel like it's just you there in that life of yours while everyone else is on a beach somewhere glamorous with their eclectic and funny group of friends. Lucky. Looks fun.

Sometimes friendship is bright like that. Sometimes it's quieter. Like for a season. Or an afternoon. Or a shared experience it feels like only you two will understand. We reach out and take care of each other in the hope we get the same care in return.

There are some friendships that shape your life entirely, life-affirming connections that hold gravity in your life, that tell you who you are. They're quiet, messy and come out in the unaesthetic moments of life, peeling a banana for you in your filthy flat when you're too weak to move. Or rushing you to the emergency room when you think you've got a life-threatening insect bite. They give you the feeling that whatever happens, someone will be there for you who's not under any oath or contract to do so. You don't have to pretend anything with these people. If you think about it, it's the most romantic thing.

As our social lives bounce between real life and splintered group chats governed by their own dynamics, our experience of friendship is far less linear and more nuanced than it used to be. It's a funny reality that the answer to our hyperconnected loneliness might actually lie in categorising our friendships more formally so we're clearer about what to expect from them, how much to give them and what we get in return.

Because we're always trying to find people who 'get' us. We might connect with many people, but to be truly understood is a rare, separate feeling altogether. It's how we're both here. In our dream world, it's how you found this book. We will find friendships, forge them, lose them and let them shape our whole lives. But in order to have them in the first place, we have to understand how to open up our lives to let them come, and let them go.

What would you do if I, like, died?

BEL: If I died what would you miss about me

LUCY: is this a cry for help

BEL: No I have my period and I'm feeling vulnerable
Vulnrey
Vuln?
Doesn't type as cute as I'd hoped

LUCY: lol no
looks short for voltaren
or the name of voldemort's son
anyway we must have synced
i put some peanut m&ms in the fridge for you

BEL: You're too good to me
Back to the missing
For example, I would miss the way you are the best person at texting me back ever to have lived
Like, I have lost track of hours messaging you
The worst of hours, the best of hours
Shakespearean, really

                                    LUCY: stop

BEL: It's so good.
It would leave a giant gap in my life
And it feels essential that you know this.

         LUCY: well if you died i would never be able to look at
                                      another aqueduct again
                       after you taught me what they were that time

BEL: Touching.
I would get the actor from Daisy Jones and the Six — you
know the one related to Elvis?
I'd hack into SYSCA and DM her
And get her to do a cover of Silver Springs to play at your
memorial

              LUCY: you're lucky because as per your request
              i've been taking cute b-roll of you to use at yours since the
                                                       moment we met

BEL: Lol that was a joke and you know it, but also could
come in handy one day so maybe don't delete
Also — please make sure there is strictly gluten-free catering
at mine
Should anything happen
I couldn't bear anyone having a coeliac reaction on the one
day meant to all be about me

                                    LUCY: what about flowers

BEL: If I so much as hear there's a geranium with a wire around it
I will be livid

                      LUCY: nooo imagine if none of our exes cry

BEL: They have to. I think that's the goal
Are you home? Where are you?

                                    LUCY: in bed
                                          where u?

BEL: Also in bed. So through the wall

                      LUCY: sorry but we are psycho

BEL: Love it
Love us
Love you

                                  LUCY: love you

BEL: PS. Just emailed you the latest words for the newsy

Close Girl Summer
By Bel

Mount Eden, Auckland, New Zealand, 2022

One blue summer, following the implosion of my time as an In Love Cool Girl with a live-in boyfriend, thought-we'd-be-together-forever boyfriend, I wound up in the camping section of an outdoors store, choosing between a single or a double airbed while Robbie Williams' 'Angels' serenaded me through the speakers overhead.

This is where one love story ends and another begins.

I buy the double for good karma and call Vee. She's heading to the airport, getting on a flight. She'll be there as soon as she can. The next day, she arrives early at my hollow apartment, her car full of camping gear and a UE Boom playing Steely Dan's 'Dirty Work'. She walks through my door, and I collapse into her arms, a weak version of myself I can't recognise. It's embarrassing. She doesn't care. I've just bought a spearmint vape. We get in the car.

'You talk, I drive,' she says as we pull out of the driveway.

We drive to the healing sky of Northland, where we meet our other friends standing in our camping section in hunting shorts, bikini tops and bare feet. Tragedy is so perfect like that, opening up all this space for people to walk into your life.

'Fucking hell,' they say and entertain me with more questions and declarations about how I'd been failed and fuck that and fuck him and other important things you need to be told by your friends when your life's falling apart. Vee, Kirsty, Eli and Jaz treat me like I've had the worst thing happen to me in the world, even though it has happened to them all too at some point. They let me cry under a blue-and-white striped sunshade in the morning and over homemade Cosmopolitans in an enamel mug at night, playing Red Hot Chili Peppers' back catalogue to keep my mind from wondering about why I'm 29, and this is happening to me, I thought I was stupid and thought I was finally immune to this. The sunshade, a Christmas present from my ex, becomes a running joke across the week, a motif in the film of our lives; flimsy and collapsing within seconds of being put up and holding on for dear life at the corners. We look like the reality TV show set of *Robinson Crusoe* if it was about single women making it out of a family campground alive. Auckland, home, where I have emails and a job and used to have my life together feels like it doesn't exist.

I'm like a baby chimp being looked after: pink drinks here, bacon butties there, Vee rubbing Voltaren into my aching back while Eli passes me her vape to hoon when the next wave of pain rolls in. A fellow camping man walks past and remarks, 'You guys are crack-up. You should film this and put it on Instagram!' Later that night, Eli hears him in the bathrooms asking a guy if his 'missus was on his level,' and if she wasn't, offering to 'go back to their campsite and help him talk to her.'

We stay for a week, sunbathing topless at secret beaches, sleep in late, plan nothing, don't speak for hours and eat oysters bought from a vendor on the motorway as the sun goes down. No one talks about work or the city, and I want to stay in that safe, soft feeling forever. In the hell of losing what I thought was everything, I lose my debit card, and Vee pays for everything on her own. I feel like I'm running up a friendship debt, but no one seems to mind looking after me, and that in its own right feels astonishing: the way women heal each other when romance fails to. There may be gender pay gaps and glass ceilings and states ruling on abortion laws, but this is a secret power women will always have, and what it's capable of will never cease to amaze me.

This is what happens when you have a Close Girl Summer. It's the rarest, most cosmic thing: a group of women who happen to be single or free at the same time and are living together for the feeling. The hard parts of life fall away for a while. You become the most tanned you've been in your life. You hit on spearfishermen. You source someone to take a new LinkedIn profile photo. You discuss taking your Miranda-style maxi skirt back to the shop. You have time back, you start doing things you used to love. You jump off rocks and take photos and mince around in pyjama shorts together, eating leftovers with plastic cutlery and drinking lukewarm water. It's your own world to live in together, and for as long as it lasts, it's the safest place to be.

In your own world is your own language, too. You develop the concept of Who Cares Moments,[5] which relieves you from responsibility for anything, particularly how things will turn out and whose fault something is. Who cares about anything? Have another drink. Dance in your kitchen with your headphones on until you're so out of breath you can't move any more. Don't reply to emails.

---

5 Who Cares Moments: Consciously choosing not to care or worry about whether a decision will ruin the rest of your life and, instead prioritising joy in the moment; frivolity over the fear of not achieving perfection.

Go on a date with that weird guy who DM'd you three months ago. Torture yourselves by rewatching *Normal People*. You describe this behaviour as Ratting Around because you couldn't imagine anything worse than having to look good or have your life together. Instead, it's you and your rats. The Rat Girls.[6] Everything aches, you have nothing to lose, and therefore nothing else matters except this. Strangers DM you and tell you they're jealous of your friendships, and you say, 'I'm lucky, I know – I've never had a love like this.'

If you've lived enough life at this point, you'll know that this time, like everything, won't last forever. So much of friendship now lives in the vortex of messages and missed calls, but the real-life-ness of a Close Girl Summer can never be matched. It's that rare moment when you and your female friends are as available to life as you are for each other. We use words like 'luck' and 'timing' to describe when friends come together like this; all the same language as romantic love, except this never gets a ceremony. You don't get celebrity-style make-up done and throw a nice party to say, 'Look at everything these people have ever done for me,' in front of everyone you love. But, in a way, that makes it even better. Even though it never lasts long, a Close Girl Summer will change the course of your life forever.

The hot days come, and somehow they go. Eventually, you must return home to the city as life does that thing it always does: it rolls on. Things get good, then they get bad, then they get good again. You cry. All the time. It's so unchic and embarrassing, but together you're able to make it funny. *Another cry today? Well done. Keep*

---

6 Rat Girling: Pushing back against the incessant pressure to be perfect by feeling completely enough in whatever you look like, whatever you're wearing and whatever you have. Minimal effort for maximum enjoyment.

up the good work. I'll be over this evening. Or did you cry at work? Hopefully, they'll feel sorry for you and you can take the afternoon off. One morning, it's so bad you call Jaz, one of your oldest friends, to come to your rescue. She arrives in ten minutes and sits in her sports gear at the end of your bed, spoon-feeding yoghurt from a bowl into your sad mouth. 'Why does this remind me of the worst bender we went on at university?' You laugh. 'You may as well hold my hair back while you're at it.'

Your neighbours think you're running a Tupperware Ponzi scheme with the revolving door of women and wine coming in and out of your house. Wine. There's so much wine. You could cater a whole wake and still have bottles left over. You're in that liminal space between cause and effect, and you're allowed to do whatever you want. The numbness is liberating.

You stay up late together on school nights, drinking in the warm light of your lounge, reading aloud horoscopes and matching exes with each others' stories, eating chips for dinner and trading back left-behind bikinis. You speak intimately about someone's breakdown, recommend doctors and apps and better ways of doing things that are imperfect but might just work. You know about each other's mothers, long-time crushes and the things you regret the most. You stand at the kitchen sink cluttered with dishes and look back into the space where you live, which is devoid of who you thought was the love of your life, but filled with something else entirely.

January burns on. Someone's breakdown gets better. Another's job refuses to pay her well. You collectively concoct a situation in which you 'Robin Hood' the company and redistribute its wealth. You befriend the woman at the nearby liquor store who reads you internet therapy infographics she's saved on Instagram and tells you you need a haircut. 'Oh honey, this one's good,' she says as she checks through your discount Chardonnay. 'The worse the pain, the more times you have to let go of it. You should print that out and put it on your fridge.'

'I will,' you lie. *I have to get to the point where this just a thing that happened, not the only thing that's happened to me,* you think as you walk out through the store's automatic doors.

You become obsessed with the same four sad songs and play them on repeat, driving around the city with the windows down. In your vision, it's the year 2000 and simpler times: you're a boomer at a winery concert in a racerback singlet, a slingback heel and a lanyard carrying a plastic cup of Pinot Grigio, remembering this song because nothing can go wrong. You've bought your house. You've paid your dues. There will be a pandemic and a president in years to come, and you'll have a lucky stack of memories to keep the fears at bay.

It's February now, and during a late-night long-distance phone call with a faraway friend, she says with aching clarity, 'You get to 30 and roll over in the night and look at the person sleeping next to you and think: you're either the love of my life or the worst pain I will ever experience.' Oh God, the stakes just get higher as you get older. You're flooded with horror visions of everyone floating away on their own blow-up love islands, and you're left on the shore like an unsuccessful contender on a dating reality TV show.

'What if it's the pain?' you ask.

'If it's the pain part – honestly, it's like the end of your life's just happened. You feel that in a way it nearly ruins your life. And then, you do what you said – you phoenix.'

Your friends stay with you even when you think you don't need them at all. You spend Saturday afternoons talking about your horny trysts, the rules you promise you're not breaking. You buy each other glass vases and an afternoon at hot pools and books by Korean philosophers that you show the liquor-store lady to prove your emotional progress. 'I like this one,' she says, pointing to a page, and tears off some of the receipt paper from the till to write the quote on the back. She says, 'You're looking better, honey,' and you wonder if it would be weird if you invited her over with the others to celebrate.

Time is running out, and you know it. You make each other watermelon salads and meet on the rocks by the sea after work. Just all appearing within minutes, as though a secret whistle's been blown and only those in tune can hear. This will be an image burned into your mind: shoeless, jerseys over your damp swimsuits, eating chips straight out of the packet, lecturing each other on how dating is a job interview (they are the candidate), telling each other 'you look like Cameron Diaz'. Telling you you're 'elite' and not to worry, even though you feel like a badly written protagonist in a Netflix special that no one wants to watch.

Slowly but surely, you build each other back up. As time creeps forward and the light wanes, you'll come out of the shower one evening to a bite in the air, the faint outlines of your bikini arching over your hips like a sweet scar, reminding you that with great pain comes great joy, and from both can come the greatest togetherness you've ever known.

There will be circumstances in your life that feel like they've robbed you of all your magic. Literally. You will feel like a hollowed-out tree with nothing left. That Close Girl Summer (doesn't it always sound like a voiceover of a college movie whenever a sentence starts like that?) showed me a person I never knew was possible. On the last night at the rocks, when it was getting dark too soon and the wind was picking up, I read aloud from my Notes app essay I'd been writing all summer, and we all cried because we'd all changed and because you get the love you deserve. And then I came home, put my wet bikini in the sink, sat down and started writing this book.

All I want from you is memes and support
By Lucy

Cynics love to tell us that strangers online are good for three things: scamming, catfishing and sending unsolicited dick pics. They've obviously never been on the receiving end of an email from someone you've never met with the subject line 'Sorry, but I feel like you'll LOVE this', containing nothing but a link to an article that uses Minions to explain the labour market. These types of online strangers – the ones who know you intimately enough to understand that Minions are the only way you're going to give up five minutes to read about the economy – are one of the true joys of the internet. Better still? There's no expectation that you'll ever meet them outside the comfort of your pyjamas.

Online friends are the antidote to the work emails and the trolls and the algorithms that make you think that everyone's off celebrating Galentine's Day while you're at home alone with a cheap red. They're the part of the internet that keeps you there because it can still be fun and low-stakes. You'll never let them down by having to cancel on them, you don't have to dress up and take public transport only to order a coffee that you don't even want because it's already 3pm, and you'll be up all night if you drink it. Hell, for those of us who are convinced we communicate better online than we do in real life, we even get to avoid small talk. Dreamy!

You won't turn to them in a crisis or call them when you've locked yourself out of your apartment, but they'll be the first to send you a niche playlist called something like 'Burnt out former gifted emotional support eldest daughter' to keep your mind off everything. Perhaps you met them at an online book club, and now you DM them solely for their thoughts on the latest edition of the trilogy you love. Or you met them on Twitter after realising you were both publicly thirsting over the same niche band, so now you watch live streams together and link each other to fandom drama only they'll care about. Maybe you met while exploring the lands of your favourite game, and now you've set a regular time to go adventuring together.

When content sharing is your love language, love from your online friends is abundant. They're from different time zones and cultures and age groups, and it's like being in a communal hostel but one where you don't have to share a bathroom. They'll teach you that an Irish Goodbye is not what you think it is and, in return, you can introduce them to the delicacy that is a bacon and egg pie. You'll teach them how to say good morning in your country's indigenous language (*mōrena*), and they'll teach you words from where they live that don't even translate to English (*trúnó:* –'the act of getting into a very private, confessional conversation with someone, usually accompanied by alcohol'). All of this because they subscribed to your newsletter.

Your online friends will remind you that the point of friendship isn't to fill a dinner table or all the beds on a hen weekend. It's not to exceed the number of people you can tag in a single photo on Instagram or to have the most speeches at your birthday. These might be ways to *perform* your friendship, but they're not the point of it. The point is having someone to understand you. To think about you. The best thing about online friends, then, is that they're thinking of you *despite* having never met you. And there's something quite beautiful about that. May your wifi be strong and your friendships stronger.

Riding around this life with you

Online. Real life. Girl friends. Boy friends. Bad friends. Anything friends. Everything friends. Bone friends. Once a year coffee at the nondescript café friends. Niche hobby, 'see you at the D&D meet up' friends. Saturday morning friends. FaceTime me from your bed with greasy slicked-back hair friends. Friday night, seven drink friends. DM dark thoughts in the middle of the night friends. Intermittent friends. Internet friends. Lost friends. Dangerous friends. Annoying friends. New friends. Never text you back but eventually show up late friends. Enduring friends. Bleed in your sheets friends. Disappointing friends. Fading friends. Dying friends. Unexpected friends. Changing friends. Always on time, never forgetting friends. Forever friends.

Who you spend your time with changes who you become.

In good company:
a taxonomy of friendship

Older friends.

Chosen family.

Male Best Friends.

Changing friends.

Best friends.

Losing friends.

Girl friends.

Older friends
By Bel

LA at night, and it's all the pictures I've ever seen and all the Californian songs I've ever heard, except I can only feel this from the 27th floor of a rented apartment. It's 2016, female vulnerability is trending, and I'm here on a freelance job with my photographer friend Sara, shooting real women in the wild wearing skincare and acting natural and beautiful. She does the pictures, and I do the words, and even though three decades separate us, we've never felt it.

We met through a mutual friend and connected immediately. I'd been writing poems while working in advertising, and Sara opened up a creative realm that I didn't know was possible. I thought work and art-making were mutually exclusive, and she showed me a way in which they could collide and gave me the confidence to try it for myself. We landed a job in LA together and spent hours talking over pots of tea in her kitchen, sharing stories about our travels and adventurous yearnings that never seemed to fit the mould of what we were meant to be doing. She'd make me whisky sours, play the same music I was listening to while we drove around doing site recces in her car, and teach me the importance of always packing things like a Turkish towel when I travelled: 'It will go anywhere and can transform into anything.' Like every talented photographer, in her work she shows a new way of seeing, and on those chaotic trips together, she showed me a new way of seeing myself.

We've just wrapped an exhausting day location-scouting in LA, and I'm sitting half-dressed on a big white bed when there's a knock at the door. It's Sara, carrying a laptop processing files from her SD card in one hand and an open pack of chips in the other.

'So I'm thinking . . .' she says, sliding her gear onto the duvet, 'Jailbreak?' It's late, maybe 10pm, and somewhere out there is the Chateau Marmont, the Hollywood sign, chaos and danger, and we want in.

'I'll get dressed.'

Five minutes later, we're side-by-side in the lobby, catching a cab to Abbot Kinney. The driver, an outrageous American man in his mid-forties, spends the whole ride telling us about his screenplay.

'Don't freak out, but I'll probably be famous soon. It's highly likely you'll look back on this car ride and say, "Oh my God, I remember that guy! I should have gotten an autograph!"'

'Ahh, but you also have no idea who you're in this car with!' Sara replies. She turns to me and says, 'We need to get you some of this American conviction.' She sees something in me I'm unable to locate: potential.

We pull up at a mezcal bar in Venice, I get a signature from the next Oscar-winning screenwriter on the back of an ATM receipt, and Sara takes a small table by the window.

'I know it's cliché, but I've felt like a girl my entire life,' Sara says, setting her drink down. 'I don't care what anyone else thinks about ageing; most parts of your spirit never change.'

'I feel part girl, part 75 years old . . . it's never . . . it's never seemed to match,' I reply. This is how we connect. In each other, we see another version of ourselves.

'How do you know you're good at what you do?' I ask. It's a question I've been turning over that I haven't been able to find the answer for.

'I don't think you do. I think you just decide to keep trying and keep making the things that feel necessary.'

We slide the night along together in a series of drinks and plates we pay for using our per diems. Sara talks at length about her own photographic travels, which she calls 'girl wandering,' and the phrase unlocks something inside me. It describes my non-linear way of living as though it is following the journey of someone magnificent who's come before me. Girlhood is so often mythologised, and for good reason: exchanges like these open up worlds within ourselves, that we let each other 'become' in. Naming this way of living transiently, freelancing along the way, helped me feel like jumping off the corporate ladder wasn't wasting my time; I was doing 'something'. I learnt more in a drink with Sara than I did in half my arts degree.

Older friends always have that transformational effect – making us want to fast forward to a time and a place where life's resolved and all the hard decisions are made. It's a tacit, earned wisdom we can bypass too easily if we don't stop long enough to listen. The night goes on, and we order more drinks and purposely lose track of time.

'Once you took a photo of me, and it was the first time I actually liked what I saw,' I admit. I sound emo, but I'm not; I'm getting drunk, it's fun and I don't care. The room fills with people in hats and the vegan California hum.

'Darling,' Sara grabs my hands across the table. 'You have to believe what I see in you. You'll look back on who you were and won't be able to believe what she did or who she was.' She sets my hands down and takes another sip. 'All the pains will slide away, and I think you'll marvel at her.'

'What do you see when you look back at your own life?' I ask.

'Someone more beautiful and curious than I ever knew at the time,' she replies. 'But we don't need to have all the answers at once. They don't come like that. Nothing can ever prepare you for each decade of your life.'

'Sara,' I'm slurring now. The mezcal's made everything feel like stars. 'You make me brave.'

'You know what? I feel the same. You keep my world from getting smaller as yours gets bigger and bigger.'

'But how do you know what to do with it all?'

'You never do,' she smiles and takes the last sip from the glass before it's cleared away. 'Sometimes you just have to lie back in the river and let it take you.' 'This . . . you . . . here . . .' she gestures around the buzzing restaurant, 'We've just got to take these chances as often as possible. They make us come alive.' She signals for the bill and pays, and we both stand up to leave.

In the Uber, Sara's phone rings. It's her husband back home. I check my own blank lock screen: an embarrassing reminder that no one is wondering where I am or what I'm doing. Out the window, the neon signs advertising psychics and foot massages speed past.

What is the future? Who will call me? How will I know? Maybe I can go anywhere and transform into anything.

In friendship, there are no contracts. There are no bloodlines or legacies, no rings or vows or babies or prenups. It's just you, knocking on each other's doors holding a half-eaten pack of chips and a look in your eyes that says in both the safest and most spontaneous way possible: let's go.

Chosen family
By Lucy

For a long time, I thought I'd marry him. Truthfully, I don't think that was ever because I was in love with him, it was more that everyone else told me that I should, and because I desperately wanted to be a part of his family. It's the classic small-town love story: we met when we were babies, and our dads worked together doing farm and farm-adjacent things. When we were 11 years old, we were put in the same class at a new school, and we were the teachers' pets. We became the class counsellors and he says I made him be the secretary at every meeting so I could do all the talking while he furiously took down all the notes. It's kinda been that way ever since.

As teenagers, we had on-again-off-again crushes on each other to pass the time. I'd embarrass myself by knocking the hubcaps off my tires on the sidewalk trying to park, and he'd embarrass himself by getting his foot stuck in between the cinema seats on our first proper date. My dad drops me off, and his dad picks me up. I know they're talking about how funny it is that the two kids who met as babies at the farm-adjacent workplace are now going to the movies together. The crushing only lasts a little while, but even when we both eventually grow up and out of it, we never grow out of each other's lives.

There is a mutual understanding that we're both 'shit at communication' when it comes to keeping in touch, which actually makes going to different universities and living in different cities easier. We each know how the other works and that the only thing that will change about us is that we use different slang words now and one of us has gotten really into politics. We're off filling our lives with new stories, and every time we get to catch up it's a race to spit it all out before we have to get back on our separate planes.

His mum is the first person to text me on my birthday every year. She compliments my hair even when I go through my pink box-dye phase. I visit her when he's not home, and she shows me her secret tattoo before anyone else in the family, because she trusts me.

One day I hear the term 'chosen family' and think that whoever coined it must have been a fly on the wall of our friendship. Watching as we sit around in their never-fully-renovated lounge while his dad shows us all his favourite X Factor performances on YouTube. Watching as we drunkenly beat his brothers at cards, again. Watching as he brings home a new girlfriend and they accidentally call her my name.

It's romantic to talk about your friends and their families becoming your own. After all, they get the best bits of you while you take home all the ugly stuff, in the same way a cool aunt gets to leave when the baby starts to cry. But it's romantic because it's a love you choose. It's not inherited. You're not part of the bloodline. Instead, you're bonded by inside jokes and secrets and an unspoken understanding that they'll be there drunkenly FaceTiming you from a family wedding because they know you'll want to see the dress. You're lucky if you love the family you're given, but you're even luckier if you find one you love enough to choose over and over again.

Male Best Friends
By Bel

In the movies, the Male Best Friend (MBF) can't get his life together. He's all like, 'I looove love, but I love myself more!' Or he's got blond frosted tips and can just never seem to make it anywhere on time. Or he's in love with you. Or he's not, but everyone thinks you're in love with him, so you should fly across the country and steal a motorbike to ruin his wedding.

None of this is what I know to be true.

What I know of Male Best Friends, not the movie ones, is that they defy all the things about men that otherwise let us down. In all the times I've been spoken over, pushed into, overworked or not looked after, I come back to him, standing in my kitchen or landing in my inbox, helping me handle and enjoy my life, with no sex in the way. His presence is forever restoring my faith in the modern man: he is my blueprint for love.

My MBF and I met when I was nineteen and still carrying around a skateboard. We'd both started working shifts at an old theatre in Wellington, which was the perfect university job; pouring Lindauer for customers in a building that was so easy to get lost 'going to get something' that no one would notice you'd been busy doing nothing until it was time to leave.

There must have been a big cricket game on that night because

I remember making a joke about Laver & Wood (the name of a cricket bat manufacturer from my hometown and the only relevant thing about the sport I knew), and he laughed so hard he nearly dropped a tray of champagne flutes on the kitchen floor. Clink. We've been part of each other's life ever since.

It's easy to mistake this trajectory for the romantic kind of love; I can see where the directors are coming from. They'd see us sitting across from one another in a restaurant and think, 'That's the chemistry we want – that's the opening shot!' But it's not.

I'm in both of his graduation photos. He's carried my life out of three flats and into two airports. We've sat side-by-side at fraught family dinners, breakups, sports matches and accidents. We've drunk cocktails with *Lord of the Rings* actors in pubs and called ambulances after nights out that lasted so long we were convinced we were going to die. We've survived natural disasters and separations and sicknesses that – when you say it all together like that – it sounds like the way you talk about the love of your life, but, as he puts it, 'You don't have to fuck everyone you love.'

Speaking of fucking, it also means we've been bystanders in the most treacherous and experimental years of each other's dating lives. The obsessive arborist. The hot artist. The acid activist. Over a decades' worth of romantic misadventures have come and gone between us. I used to fetishise romance because I saw it as a way to escape myself, but my MBF's presence has always had the opposite effect, making me want to come back properly to myself each time, making me feel like I shouldn't need to abandon who I was in the first place. There are very few people in this world who can say anything to you, and you trust them enough to truly believe them.

MBFs are the kind of friendship that reveals how you can

love someone in such an uncomplicated way that all other love around it starts to seem straightforward. Like gravity, or the way ships float, or the way your phone can never take good photos of the moon. It just is. They just are. It's a kind of anti-love love the movies don't know what to do with (But who gets together in the end?! What do they do now, just *hang out*?!!) It's what therapists call 'unconditional'. It's what married couples swear they go by. It's the rule at which all harmonious things in the world operate.

He is having a baby soon. Whenever I feel disenfranchised by the world, I think about him and his partner making a new, mini version of themselves, bringing about all this new hope at a time when it's so easy to lose it. I know this sounds like something someone would stand up at a christening and say while there's a climate change protest happening outside, but it's true. He is what I measure love against. He is how I know it's real. He makes me feel glad I exist.

Changing friends
By Bel

In the beginning, it's a lot like falling in love.

We're 19 and both dressed like Phoebe Buffay swallowed in synthetic knits and floral dresses from a roadside op-shop. We're in the black mouldy kitchen of an avocado-coloured flat, in a burger shack, on a grey beach, having a long week, and nothing could be more perfect than being there together. In the beginning, there's us two. And then there is everybody else.

In the beginning, it's all about secrets and chaos. About leaving home and setting up versions of our own homes. Sometimes to live, but other times just to wind up on the other side of each others' beds after a cheap stir-fry and a late night pushing pixels around a screen, wondering what will become of us.

In the beginning, it's experimental hair colours (red) and noisy gigs (always on a Tuesday night, always terrible). It's making out with strangers and vomiting in the alleyway next to the discount bookstore where one of us works on Sundays and the other visits, delivering hot hangover carbs. It's perusing ASOS, which has just been invented, figuring out each other's 'style' and perfecting it to a fine art while stoned on a bath towel at the Botanical Garden on a Sunday. In the beginning, it's the opposite of loneliness.

In the middle, we develop the concept of 'Dream'. We play it when we get home late from parties and lie in each others' beds, taking turns to outline dream scenarios for each others' lives. She's an Egyptologist on assignment in the desert. I'm a poet on a boat on the Amazon. A professor falls in love with her, but she's too elegant to care. I invent a new famous typeface. She's chic and accomplished, and something great happens where I never have to work again. We play 'Dream' when we're sad. We play it when we're lonely. We play it when we come home drunk and alive with the possibility of what we could become. 'Dream' is how we make maps for each others' lives.

In the middle is change. One of my 'Dreams' somehow works out because, in the middle, we both get a creative break. She's designing a poetry book, and I'm writing it. She's becoming smarter by the day, and I'm becoming braver with my visions of where I want to go and what I think is possible. In the middle, we spend weekends together, working for hours side-by-side in silence, printing and scanning and stitching things together. In the middle is devotion.

There is no ending, but there's an end to the beginning. People warn you this might happen. No, you say, that's for other people; that's *not us*. They make films about our kind of friendship, we'll be like this forever. But that thing that happens to people who use that word ('forever') as though time will never run out happens to us. We move to opposite ends of the world. We get busy. Get jobs. Fall in love. Become entangled in other universes with other rules and languages. We run out of time for one another.

In the end (the ending of sorts), we lose our gravitational pull. I think I'm no longer me because I'm no longer needed the way I used to be. It's a sharp grief that's embarrassing to describe: like looking up at a race track and being left behind. I know losing, and I know triumph, but I haven't felt a gap in my life quite like it. It's like the opposite of love, which is its absence.

In the end, it's messages with no questions, and one-line replies your parents use like 'good', 'busy' and 'tired'. In the end, it's finally admitting things are no longer what they were. In the end, it feels embarrassing that I clung on so long in the first place when everyone is entitled to their own life, I just didn't know friendships could change the same way relationships do. These are quiet reconciliations I work through over time.

In the very end, it will be years later, and we'll both have lives and proper haircuts and the same skin problems. We'll find ourselves the night before a wedding in a shabby chic bedroom trying on our silk dresses hanging in the doorway, half-drunk on a bottle of tomorrow's wine and say, 'Everything's changed, and I still love you, just in a different way.'

Best friends
By Lucy

Unless there's an occasion, you probably don't hug. Large displays of affection are for people who are new to this, but you two have been going steady for a while now. When you were younger, you made up a handshake that made everyone feel left out, and that was the point. You wanted other people to want this. You grew out of the jeggings trend but never out of each other. And even though it's been a forever thing, you'll probably struggle to find a photo of the two of you together to share on their birthday, but that's okay because you don't need to prove anything to social media.

You'll copy each other's bad hairstyles in solidarity, even if the new colour washes you out. They'll borrow your glasses and ID because if there's one person who is allowed to steal your identity on a night out, it's them. You'll be each other's only friends for a while, waiting to hit your peaks together. You'll hit them at different times, but you won't be jealous of each other. They'll know when you're spiralling and that they can't talk you out of it. Instead, they'll text whoever's nearest you and arrange for you to be spied on from afar. They'll become a part of your family, sharing cigarettes with your mum and taking the piss out of your dad. One of your brothers will call them his sister, one will profess to want to marry them, and the other will have to carry them home when you both get too drunk one night.

They'll be close, even when you're distant. They'll tuck letters away for you to read on planes or buses even though that's 'not something you guys do.' They'll cheer for you in crowds and on stages or when you buy a new jacket that you can't afford. They'll be the one casting the spotlight on you even when it should be on them.

For months and then years and then decades you'll lie in new beds in far-off cities rehashing the same tales you've been telling since high school, with every new detail you remember giving you an excuse to take it from the top again. You've been romanticising your lives long before that became a buzzword on the internet, with stories that last far longer than the ones that only exist for 24 hours on Instagram. Social media is where fleeting friendships live. This is not that.

One night, when you're living further away from them than you've ever been, you'll get a little bit drunk and wish they were with you. The alcohol will start making you do that terrible self-reflection thing, and you'll type them a message, asking why they stuck around for so long, even in the years when you felt like a difficult friend to keep. They'll simply respond, 'It was worth it.'

Losing friends
By Bel

Homestay, Patiala, India, January 2012

I'm running out the door of our homestay when it happens. Our ride for a day trip from Patiala to Amritsar is late and, with the extra time, I log onto our host family's laptop to check the news from home. Among the headlines about partying rugby league players, hibiscus-print tankinis and summer festival line-ups reads:

ELEVEN DEAD IN CARTERTON BALLOON CRASH

I remember that day in the café. I remember Alexis' plans for the summer while I'd be away. Everything goes very quiet and very still for an indeterminate period of time.

Years later, this experience of reading about human devastation right next to how to style this summer's sarong will have become the main way we discover news. It's a concertina of frivolity and devastation that swooshes past us in one scroll, compressing the good with the bad so quickly we don't have time to fully register what we've just seen. Experts will gather in an academic conference and coin this everyday part of modern living as 'context collapse.'

University café, Wellington, New Zealand, 2011

Six months earlier, Alexis, Olivia and I meet in our nylon-carpeted university café after class, taking turns sipping coffee and acting out the dramatic stories of our lives. Alexis and I met as teenage theatre nerds at a youth drama school, and immediately connected over our love for losing ourselves on stage. We hadn't hung out enough to get close yet, but she had this honeyed disposition that drew in everyone around her, putting them immediately at ease. Olivia was dating Alexis' brother Ben, and once we worked that out, we soon all became friends. One afternoon, late to our coffee date, Alexis came running in, cheeks flushed pink, almost unable to speak. She'd accidentally discovered the tickets for a hot air balloon ride on her boyfriend's desk and she has called us to hash out the best way to pretend she hasn't. It felt like the basis for a plot line of an early 2000s rom-com.

'OK, again, again, but act more surprised!' I shriek. Alexis walks backwards from the table, shaking her face to reset it to put on a slightly different character, the way we learned at drama school, and sits back down.

'Ahhh! I can't believe it!' she gasps breathily, her sweet face lit up as she clutches the napkins she's using as a prop for the ticket envelope. We cackle into our lukewarm mochachinos.

'It's actually so cute,' says Olivia.

'Oh my God, what if he proposes?!' I ask, 'Gosh, oh my gosh,' I add hastily.

Alexis and her boyfriend are Christian. I don't fully understand how that shows up in a relationships when you're 19, but I hear the grand gestures that are lacking in my own agnostic life are more normal in theirs. Her eyes lift up from her cup and transform into a Powerpuff Girl – the way all young women in love look. The way naivety does.

'You never know what might happen,' she smiles and takes a sip.

Mount Cook flat, Wellington, New Zealand, 2011

In our first photography class at university, a goth tutor we nicknamed 'Skeletor' because of all her skeleton-inspired accessories, said, 'I don't want to see any photos of the beach, your grandmother or your friends. Go and get an imagination, for fuck sake.' I'd never felt more provincial in my life.

I had already been thinking about a trip like the one to India, and the prophetic words of a skull-clad photographer were the thing that did it: I had to go and make my world bigger. I wanted to forget my 19-year-old's pains and try to understand life in the chaos of somewhere else. It was 2011, and *Eat Pray Love* had debuted in cinemas the year before. Spiritual tourism had taken off, and women were being encouraged en masse to dump men, return the appliances they'd been gifted for their anniversaries and go try to be happy somewhere else. I chose India.

My flatmate Rhi decided to join me, and we found a volunteer site based in a Punjabi city six hours north of New Delhi that would have us over the Christmas break. One Saturday afternoon, we walked down to a travel agent and drained the savings we'd made from pouring lukewarm Sauvignon Blanc at theatre bars and running a teenage skate park and bought our flights. It was the most impractical thing I'd ever done.

Travelling was so new and surreal to me. It felt like something an exotic and accomplished woman would have been doing her whole life; traits I thought a journalist needed when she was out in the field in a high-waisted black pant, pushing for the truth and fooling men into giving her tip-offs that would break news stories and later be turned into an award-winning documentary.

It was also the time before everyone had the internet on their phones and vlogs and reels that got you right down to the detail of which bunk bed to reserve in the hostel down the long driveway. Instead, we printed off a giant map of India and Blu-Tacked it in the damp hallway of our flat, opening our doors and looking at it each morning, wondering which of its lines we'd cross, what we'd see and just how far we'd be able to go. It was a time before you could ever really know what you were getting yourself into.

Patiala to Amritsar, India, 2012

I see the headline, and the hours that follow are a senseless blur. I tell Rhi what's happened in a stutter. Our tuk-tuk arrives, and the next thing I know we're in the back seat of a car speeding north, beelining towards the Pakistani border through colour and dirt and people and dust. It's state election time, and there are men with AK-47s stopping traffic and tapping on windows, searching boots, looking for bribes. At a checkpoint, a gun's pointed at my head through the glass, and Mani, our guide and driver, says, 'Don't worry! We're fine!' We drive off. 'Also – we're going to the home of God,' as he looks at me in the rearview mirror. I can't believe it.

By the time we arrive at the Golden Temple, it's turning dark, the perfect light to be there, although I can't feel a single thing. I can't stop thinking about Alexis in that hot air balloon hovering off the ground. *What was it like? To know it was all about to be over? Did it hurt? Could it be stopped? What did she think about? Why the hell am I here?* She was an infinitely better person than I was, and yet I was alive, and she was dead. I wonder if there is a God. If so, I wonder where the hell she is. Is she here? Seems like a lot of gold in this temple to waste on mere mortals. I need her to stop listening to everyone else's problems for a second and explain herself. Mani ushers us inside.

We sit in our Punjabi outfits along the edge of the moat surrounding the temple, which is covered in tiny joyous mirrors and gold. Other travellers are talking and laughing in awe, and all I can think about is logistics. The height the balloon reached before it fell. The crash into the powerlines. The fire. The last breath. The ripple effect. I close my eyes and blink back tears. It feels insane to feel this engulfed in grief for someone I could barely write an acrostic poem about. I try to leave a fragment of her memory here, among the gold and the peace. I want to message her parents and tell them about doing so, but I don't even know what I would say. I didn't even know her well enough for them to know who I am. This is not my grief, but I feel it anyway.

That night, we get home late, and I can't sleep, so I do something I never do when I'm so far away because it feels like an admission of failure: I call my dad. It's early back home, but I wonder if he's up in his own insomnia, worrying about the cattle or the forecast or his own feelings we'll never speak of.

'Dad?' I creak. I feel like a girl in a storybook.

'Mouse, what's wrong?' It must be alarming to receive a call at that time; I can hear it in his voice. But he's up (I hear him sit up, imagine his back straighten, the lump rise in his throat).

'My friend . . . there's been an accident. She's – she's dead.'

It's the first and only time things change like this between us.

The line goes quiet, like white noise, but I know he's still there on the other end. After about a minute, he starts speaking softly about losing his best friend, hit by lightning out on his horse right before his wedding.

'What are the odds?' he says, 'I just don't know how we make sense of these kinds of things, but we have to . . . it's all we've got.' I hear him take a sip of his coffee and set it back down on the kitchen bench. 'That's why I don't believe in any of that God bullshit,' he says. I decide not to tell him where I've just been.

New flat in Aro Valley, Wellington, New Zealand, 2012

Rhi and I arrive back to a new university year in Wellington at the height of summer. It's the day before my 20th birthday. I've missed Alexis' funeral; instead, I watched photo albums uploaded on my newsfeed through the same broken laptop screen I learned about her death on. We rent a falling-down flat with friends in the city's notoriously dank suburb, dance in dresses at parties, submit assignments, make lentil bakes in our mouse-infested kitchen; all those simple, happy things. The news runs other reports. More bad and good things happen. I try to squash down the grief I don't feel entitled to. Leaving the house feels difficult. I can't reconcile these two realities: being back here, living, and what I'm catching up with, having watched from so far away. It's like I've left my body back in another world. Oh no – that's what dying is.

Later that year, in the car on the way to a 21st birthday party, some friends get into a car accident, swerve right on the road and Fliss doesn't make it out alive. Fliss, the beautiful photographer with the red lips and long hair catching the wind behind her. I can't believe it. I'm working for the university magazine and am accidentally one of the first to find out. As soon as I get the phone call, I get in my car and drive to our friend Alice's house, where we sit in her bed, tipping gin into cups of tea with our mouths open, waiting for everyone to get back to the city so we'll know what to do next. It's so dark, and cold, and once again, nothing makes sense.

We sit in rumpty flats with fairy lights on around the tables, our knees touching, hearts falling out of our bodies, regaling random memories that are growing in our chests like helium balloons. We look back over Fliss' photos. We talk about the way she captured the world. I watch my friends fly to Dunedin for her funeral, and the university rector give a speech at her memorial service. The following days and weeks are filled with Facebook posts and status updates. It's a kind of terror, knowing what's possible in life, no matter how hard you try to safeguard yourself from what goes wrong. Things go wrong whether you're a good person or not, and this feels particularly difficult to accept. It's only after months and months of watching that the grief starts to properly sink its teeth in. I will be reminded of this feeling every time I get into a mode of transport for the rest of my life. Some of us get to go on living and we're the ones who must make the most of it.

The years that follow, everywhere

Watch, watch, watch: we watch so much now we can't work out whether feelings are our own or manufactured by simply just seeing it all, all the time. Online, we call watching 'impressions'. Literally, the act of having something pressed into you, or in advertising, a campaign trying to capture your attention flashing before your eyes. An artist captures an 'impression' when no other accurate representation is possible. We describe young people as 'impressionable'. All these things we're watching, they press themselves into us in the subtlest and sharpest ways, often without us even knowing. It's up to us to decide what shape they take and how they live inside of us: the mould they're making in our lives.

During that cursed year, amidst all the watching and the losing, Olivia and I meet whenever we can. She teaches me how to surf on the coast near her house, balancing on her board, one hand shielding the sun, watching waves crash time and time again into the cold sea. She is watching her partner grieve his sister. I am watching the ache of Alexis' mum, watching us make lunch in their kitchen, watching how we get to keep on living while her daughter doesn't.

After losing, there is always watching. The watching goes on forever. We watch the course of our own lives and chart them against what could have been: *is this what they would have done with theirs? Is this enough? Are they up there somewhere, watching over us?*

In the end, when we all turn into birds, all we can ask for is to fly back over our own lives and know, whether something happened to us or we saw it happen to somebody else, we did everything we could.

Girl friends

You on my lock screen. My phone when it calls. The seven-minute voice note, so you know it all. The cute shit. The bad bits. Everything we don't even need to say. Sorry, again, for the total essay. Your note on my bed. Never being left on read. That whole summer. Our secrets. The evenings that left us sleepless. Having crushes that need stalking. Being together and not talking. Late nights. Hydrolites. The calmness of knowing your advice is always right. My clothes that you wore. Your shoes, unbuckled, still lying on my floor. Screenshots. Our mistakes. Running commentary from our first dates. All my secrets that you know. Every debt that I owe. How many times do I say this before it is too much? I love you with all my skin and bones.

CHAPTER 4

The part where someone you love dies

*Dying, losing and
what's it like to watch it.*

Losing someone is gaining access to a whole world you didn't want
By Lucy and Bel

What is losing?

At its very simplest, losing is something minus something. It's a deficit, like a bad maths equation or a gap between steps that causes a chasm and a sharp intake of breath. It also begs a bigger question:

What is it to 'have' in the first place?

'Having' is why we wake up each day hoping for more. It's how we even know what more is. More excitement, more living, more moments doubled over in hilarity and, of course, more time.

To have is to love someone or something, to know them (however closely or fleetingly), and for this to take up enough space in our lives that they leave a gap when they're gone. To have is why some things just make sense. To lose is its undoing.

This is the part about the undoing.

It's about the things we can't predict nor control, no matter how much we try. The aches we can't protect ourselves from, the talismans we carry and the ungodly prayers we send. It's why sitting in the crowd of a wedding reception next to a family fighting about their pool renovations makes you want to rip your shoes off and run. It's why going to places that have lost so much helps you put your own life into perspective. It's why you get addicted to lying awake, watching anything on your phone in the dark to keep your mind from turning over, wondering 'what if?'

And, most importantly, it's about what comes afterwards.

Losing divides the world into two: people who know this feeling and people who don't. This part is for all of you. It's about the unfathomable and figuring out how to live with it.

Aftermath
By Lucy

Lisbon, Portugal, October 1st, 2023. Four years after

It's 10am and I'm scrolling on Pinterest trying to find a quote I can post on Instagram about death that doesn't feel grim or cringe or like it's been said a million times before. I'm doing this because today is a Hard Day for me, and I don't want people in my life to feel bad about forgetting to reach out. The only thing worse than feeling obliged to reply to someone who's let you know they're 'thinking of you' is feeling obliged to reply to someone who's apologising that they weren't. Thinking about Pinterest or DMs or Instagram feels like a fucking ridiculous thing to be doing on the anniversary of your little brother's death, but no one tells you what you're supposed to do. I close the apps, deciding that reading a bunch of comments about how 'the good die young' is probably not going to make this day any easier, and instead, I think about the lake we grew up at. Jimmy and I had a game we loved to play there, where we'd each grab the heaviest rock we could find and walk along the muddy floor for as long as we could each hold our breath. Each time, in the moments between dropping the rock and reaching the surface, I'd have the terrifying thought that I would pop up, look around for him, and realise I was alone. Now I know what that's like.

Don't let your parents google the Rickshaw Run

The website describes it as 'easily the least sensible thing to do with two weeks. There's no set route, no backup and no way of knowing if you're going to make it. The only certainty is that you *will* get lost, you *will* get stuck and you *will* break down.'

I couldn't tell you what about that description enticed me into the idea of racing across India. All I know is that back then, I didn't have a reason to be scared. On the weekend of my 21st birthday, I made it my mission to recruit the only two people I wanted to do the Rickshaw Run with: my little brother, Jimmy, and one of my best friends, Josh. The boys took less convincing than our parents. After almost a year of planning, fundraising and reminding ourselves that life was here to be lived, we were on our way.

India, August 2019

I'll admit that maybe we were a bit naive going into this. After saying goodbye to Mum, Dad and my brothers Nick and Ben, the boys and I endured a gnarly few days of travel, only to arrive in Kochi, India, and face some of the worst floods I've ever seen. After some drying out, we met our rickshaw: a bright yellow lemon with a smiley face on the front. Jimmy and Josh taught me how to drive it, we went and bought what we'd been told would be our essentials – things like jerry cans and zip-ties – and we boarded a boat to the opening night party. None of this was like anything we'd ever done before, and we were intoxicated by that. Jimmy was nervous, in the way anyone would be at 18, so I stayed sober to look out for him. When we got back to our hostel, he leant over the top bunk and repeatedly told me that he'd had the best night of his life, drunkenly sending our family a photo captioned 'Lucy and I are best friends.' This photo would become one of my most treasured possessions.

The race began, and we fell into our new roles. Jimmy was the best driver of the three of us, so he took the windy roads. Josh made the playlist and kept the morale high, and I, for the most part, was on map duty. We hit our stride a few days in. Unlike most of the other teams, we hadn't had a single issue with our rickshaw and were quietly confident that luck was on our side. Jimmy discovered he loved chai and the smell of jasmine. We played cricket with a bunch of local kids, and he caught them out with his 'soft hands'. Josh was warming up to his bucket showers and getting bolder with his food choices. I was just happy to be along for the ride with my brothers-in-arms.

Jimmy had always been fascinated by dams. The lake where we used to play the rock game was bookended by two of the biggest dams in the country, so when we saw one coming up on the next day's route, we diverted to it. We pulled up, and Jimmy carefully photographed it, the way he did with everything he loved, and we decided that if we wanted to keep stumbling upon things like this, we needed to be off the beaten track. And so it was settled: no more motorways from now on. It wasn't long after we'd made that decision and Josh had taken over the driving that Jimmy got a headache I instantly knew wasn't a headache.

It takes a lot for a dam to burst. A natural disaster, a freak accident, a build-up of pressure. What was happening in Jimmy's head was all three.

Google Maps. Knowing there's a hospital closer than this. Why did we leave the motorway? Holding onto Jimmy so he doesn't fall out of the Rickshaw. Directing Josh. Convincing them both it's a migraine. Knowing it isn't. Arriving. Screaming. Not being understood. Trying to lift him. Waiting. A brain aneurysm, they tell us. Surgery. Calling home. Not being able to talk. Hanging up in case we get a call from the hospital to go and buy equipment so the doctors can continue operating. Brain scans in the basement. Being shown them in tiny dark rooms. Not knowing how to make sense of them. ICU. His hands tied to the hospital bed. Days passing. Josh on the phone about travel insurance. Thank God for him. Getting worse. Mum arriving. Dad arriving. Getting better. Getting worse again. No one knowing what's wrong this time. Evacuation number one. New hospital. New week. His voice for the first time in a while. Leg movement. Precious conversations written down in my Notes app. More weeks. Another evacuation, this time to New Zealand. The doctor and nurse who flew in to help. An aggressive search of his wheelchair by security. Cuddles in a hotel bed in Singapore. Another plane. An emergency in mid-air. The ambulance meeting us on the runway. Vomiting in the airport. I thought things would be better in New Zealand? A hospital where they speak English. Fist bumps with his brothers. More weeks. Things getting worse again. Learning what antibiotic resistance means. Explaining it to my family. Last-ditch meds from Australia. Waiting. That room. That decision. Learning what palliative care means. Family visits. Friend visits. Crosswords. Laughter. Tears on his pillow. 'Young hearts don't want to stop.' More waiting. Holding his hand. The scent of bacon-and-egg pie. Spending his 19th birthday dying. Snowing at the lake. A final breath. Kissing his cold forehead. Relief.

Home, October 2019

After he died, we brought him home to spend a few nights in his old room. There he was, two doors down from me again, surrounded by his high school photography assignments and posters of his favourite cricketers. His Ferrari-red coffin sat on top of the duvet that I used to piss him off by climbing onto on Saturday mornings before he got up for the day. This annoyed him so much that in the end, we had to make an agreement: I was allowed to stay for the duration of one *Family Guy* compilation video, and then I had to get out. I wish I'd taken note of the last time I did that.

One thing the movies get right is that people will show up at your door with lasagne and sympathy. His friends came, and I took them through to see him. My friends came, and I did the same. Afterwards, we'd sit on the floor in circles and try to fill the silence of him in the next room. During this time, the most helpful thing someone could do was be there, with no expectation of being recognised for it. Sending texts that needed no reply. Showing up for a coffee that went cold without being touched. Hugging you, but letting your arms stay pressed to your sides because they know you don't have the energy to lift them. These are the things you do when there is nothing else to do.

You don't get long between losing and commemorating. There are funeral plans to be made, speeches to be written, photos to be compiled and discussions to be had about whether we should all post about it on Facebook or if we should just share Dad's post.

The music was left solely for the kids to arrange, and there could only be one artist for the main event: Kanye West. Kanye was the star on top of our Christmas tree and the soundtrack to Jimmy's life. His latest album was meant to come out on Jimmy's

19th birthday, so each day during that final month, my brothers would tuck their phones under his hospital pillow and have it lightly playing '*Ye*' as we waited for the new album to drop, thinking it might bring a miracle with it. He never did get to hear that album.

Does Kanye have a funeral-esque song? Who cares. Nick, Ben and I sat on Jimmy's bed and started going through the discography to pick the perfect tune for the midsection of a funeral.

'Runaway'

Pros: One of the classics with a strangely perfect outro for a funeral.
Cons: The boomers in attendance might not appreciate us toasting the douchebags, assholes, scumbags and jerk-offs right now.

'Can't Tell Me Nothing'

Honestly? It would have been iconic, but we couldn't have people spending the entire duration of the photo compilation wondering where they'd heard it before, only to realise it was the song from *The Hangover*.

'All of The Lights (Interlude)'

Close. Too haunting.

'Only One'

I'd known from the moment we found out he was dying that I would sing this one for him earlier in the service. Off the table.

'Ghost Town'

A song about how nothing hurts anymore and how we'll always be the kids we used to be? Perfect.

Losing means holding on. To old messages. To the sports they loved. To the music you once begged them to swap for your music on long car journeys. Jimmy died before Kanye announced his bid for president or divorced Kim Kardashian. Jimmy never had to consider whether to separate the art from the artist or if he'd be cancelled for still liking him today. I hate that I feel obliged to tell the story of my dead brother every time a Kanye song comes on one of my playlists, to caveat why I can't let his music go either. The things we hold on to become part of the treasure box we build for our loved ones, and no one is allowed to dictate what goes in or comes out.

    At his funeral, I talked about how he was the best of us all. He was the one to pick me up from the airport at every uni break, the one who took our little brother to his first party. He kept me company on the phone three nights a week as I walked home in the dark from my babysitting job. He talked to my older brother about rocket ships and how to renovate a van. He took drone photos of farms Dad was trying to sell. He helped Mum find a house when she and Dad separated. He pulled his friends' cars out of rivers or delivered them petrol when they ran out in the middle of nowhere. He rarely asked for anything, buying and wrapping his own Christmas presents and pretending to be surprised when he opened them on Christmas Day. People love to say that the best is still yet to come. How can that be true when I've just told everyone that the best of us is gone?

After making that speech, someone told me that they thought I should run for prime minister one day because of how I 'held it together'. I couldn't believe that was their takeaway from all of this. If I wasn't at my little brother's funeral, this comment would have made a really good tweet, I thought, and sensed that I'm the worst person alive for thinking that.

The months after

After the funeral, you'll have about four months of people checking in on you before they go back to their own lives, and you'll find that it's actually a relief when they do. You'll spend a lot of time trying to make other people feel comfortable about what happened and hear yourself saying things like 'they had a great life!' or 'I'm okay, really!' more than you feel you should. Your friends will tell you that you don't have to do that, but you don't know what else you're meant to say.

You'll think a lot about what they won't get to see. Like their favourite celebrity going off the rails or how that business you started with your best friends is going. You'll decide to delete your Instagram because you don't want people to be able to reach out to you anymore or see the photos of them that existed when they were here and you were happy. You'll live through a global pandemic and wonder what they would think of the world these days. You'll realise that they'll never have a 21st birthday or meet the love of their life or your brothers' girlfriends. You'll wonder if they'd have ever grown into liking olives or brussel sprouts or wine or any of those things that come with age. Every day, you will have a new revelation, and it will turn you inside out.

The years after

In the years after, other people's memories become your greatest gift. A friend of theirs might message you with a photo they found in their camera roll that you'd never seen, and you'll stick it on your fridge. An old teacher might send you something they wrote when they were younger, and your mum will cry. Their old employer might give you a drawing they'd done on a Post-It note on a slow day, signed with their name and the date, and you'll turn it into a keychain. Let these stories find you, and let the hope that more of them exist get you through the years.

In the years after, you will be told, time and time again, that you've gained a kind of perspective on the world that not many other people have. You know that missing them means they had a life worth living, that their absence is great because they were. But these romantic ways of putting it will piss you off before they bring you peace, because losing them was not worth gaining this perspective. Nothing is.

In the years after, death will make you narcissistic. Some nights, you'll be kept awake wondering why this had to happen to you. To them. Why not someone else? This doesn't make you a bad person. It also doesn't last forever.

In the years after, you will feel like you're grieving wrong because it didn't come in stages for you like the internet said it would. In fact, you're not sure if grief 'comes' at all or if it's just in you now, like lead in your bones, making sure you never feel light on your feet again.

Your life after

You'll wonder what used to occupy your brain before you knew death, and what other people spend their time thinking about. You'll sit down to watch a TV show with friends, and someone will die in it. They'll turn to you and say that they're sorry, they didn't realise, and you'll feel awkward. You'll only know 90 per cent of the *Hamilton* soundtrack because you skip all the songs about his son dying every time. You'll meet someone new and pray they don't ask you about your siblings.

People will complain about frivolous things, and you'll get irrationally angry. How can they complain about their favourite wine being out of stock when you've had someone ripped away from you forever? This anger will soften. So will you.

You will be changed in ways you won't expect, like having to google how far away you are from a hospital everywhere you go. You'll accept that this is just something about you now. You'll meet a nurse on a night out and thank them profusely for their work, wondering why the hell they aren't paid more. You'll think about how you'd become one if you weren't so freaked out by needles.

None of it is ever going to make sense. People will talk about things they've read or heard or seen, and you'll want to tell them that grief is nothing like that. Grief is walking down the street and having to slide your sunglasses on over your tears because the way the sun feels today reminds you of when you were kids together.

Death will continue to show you that life is fragile but that you are strong. Strength is having to look at your phone when it serves you a memory of them on a random Tuesday. Strength is when your family makes a new group chat without them. Strength is seeing their social media accounts become tributes. Strength is having a graduation party that they were supposed to be at. Strength is feeling their absence at every occasion, forever. Strength is knowing that you're never going to feel as happy as you were when they were here, but trying anyway. Strength is continuing to run your business because they'd want you to. Strength is stepping away when the misery vortex sucks you in and coming back when it spits you out. Strength is letting grief become your heart's compass to help you make sense of the world. How you move through it. How you navigate it. Who you are within it. Strength is being at the centre of it all, with everyone watching, especially them.

Trying to be here, trying not to freak you out, trying to show I care
By Bel

En route to Penha de França, Lisbon, Portugal, August 2023

Two years after Jimmy died, Luce and I met and quickly became friends. Soon after that, we started writing and podcasting together; her running SYSCA and me moonlighting for it on the side of my day job. It's a unique kind of closeness these kinds of collaborations demand; often out of office hours, often unmatched by many of your other relationships and often demanding a creative vulnerability not everyone gets to see. Finding someone who's obsessed with things as much as you are makes you feel like anything's possible and, when it happens, you have to run at it with wild abandon. In our early mornings scheming about our projects together, I could see the grief carefully filed within Luce like a container with the lid closed shut. Occasionally, we'd talk about it when we swapped Hard Stories, but the grief never spilled over the edge. When our book deal came through and I had the outlandish idea to go to Portugal to write it, we both wanted to leave for a similar reason: to find a place with no memories of who we were or the aches we'd experienced. We wanted newness and the perceived perfection that came with it. It's fun to test naivety for as long as life lets you.

We found an apartment at the bottom of a hill in Penha de França, where if you stood on the street and looked down, you could see marshmallow-coloured houses pointing to the Tagus river, and if you looked up, you'd see the high yellow walls of Cemitério do Alto de São João, Lisbon's largest cemetery. I landed weeks before Luce, and on the day I picked her up from the airport, we stopped at the traffic lights close to our new place. There was a heatwave and the windows of the car were down, and we were both in that adrenaline haze of moving to a foreign city and feeling high on every angle of its newness, wanting to know everything about every part of it as fast as possible.

'What's that?' she asked, pointing to the walls.

'The cemetery. Kinda weird, kinda beautiful, right?' You could see ornate statues poking out the top of the walls like candles. 'It's how I've been orienting myself back to our place,' I said, drawing an 'L' shape on the seat between us to explain the way the streets intersected. 'It also means we can get cheap flowers all the time.' I was holding a welcome bouquet of purple daisies I'd bought from a small store selling flowers for headstones. She smiled and went quiet, turning to look back out the window. I realised what I'd done, which was to bring up what she had lost the second she arrived in a new place hoping to get as far away from that feeling as possible. The lights changed. The car shifted back into gear, and we pretended nothing happened, joyfully heaving her suitcases up the narrow staircase to the new chapter of our lives, grief slipping like a card under the door behind us.

Not long after moving, Lucy's birthday and the anniversary of

Jimmy's death arrive – the two falling within a few days of each other. It's such a strange feeling as a friend, knowing the intimate turnings of someone's aches and not being able to do a single thing about them. You begin to feel them too, as though you've lost someone you never got to meet, who lives so presently in a person who is such a big part of your everyday existence. I want to offer something that's not a tiny square book of poems about grief written by men in 1919, so I find an orange seersucker shirt with an embroidered duck (Jimmy's favourite) on the front in a second-hand store and wrap it in tissue paper with a ribbon I'd brought from home. Luce cries (rare) and wears it on her birthday trip, where we take the train to the beach and swim in Cascais' blue sea coves and slosh back wine over a giant fish at lunch. An older couple nearby laughs at us, impressed, they say, that two young-looking women are having so much fun on a weekday when, theoretically they should be slaving away in their office jobs. These are the pleasures of working on the internet, we say. Besides, it's a working lunch. It doesn't look like it, but we are always working.

We're happy, uncertain about everything, but trying to figure it all out. It's an exciting, liminal space to be in because anything can happen. Sometimes, that's the problem, though. Anything. Even on the good days, there's always something that's both not there (Jimmy) and there (grief) that I can't do anything about. It's as though at any minute, disaster could strike again in a way that's totally out of our control. I watch and try to talk around this feeling without sounding like a school guidance counsellor or someone who's done an eight-part life coaching course on YouTube. We get home as the sun's just beginning to set, trailing sand all through our apartment and not caring, laughing about how much we both hate birthdays or making big deals about any day at all. One hangs out the towels while the other showers. I put a carafe of water to cool in the fridge, and the day is over. Both our bedroom doors are shut, but I know Luce is in there, through the wall, trying to find the right way to feel about another year living.

There's nothing you can say to help someone wrestle with their grief. We push it down, it comes back up again. We open the box, and the tears spill all over the edge. It's such a helpless, listless feeling: that all you can do is sit and listen and overcompensate when the car gets too hot and you're stopped outside a goddamn cemetery. The best-case scenario is that they let you in enough to wrap up in a cheap blanket next to them and re-watch an entire season of a TV show where nothing really happens, because you know the portal into a simpler world is sometimes all they need. Sometimes, there are answers. But mostly, there's just time that needs to pass, with you never completely understanding but still turning up to try.

Things I've done for no explicable reason after losing my brother
By Lucy

- Ditched the nice beer garden everyone went to after his funeral to sit on top of a grotty car park with all my friends instead.
- Gone on an annual capo bender (capitalism bender, to support both the local economy and my emotional wellbeing) where every year on the anniversary of his death, I get to buy whatever I want, no questions asked.
- Bought his strange favourite drink (Canadian Club whisky and dry ginger ale) to band practice and made everyone drink it while we toasted him.
- Put his old teddy bear up on the dashboard whenever I'm on a road trip so it can see the scenery he used to love.
- Continued to send him photos and messages and memes because even though he's missing, I won't let him miss out.
- Became obsessed with Formula 1 because it's something he used to love. Watched races with Dad and my brothers while our favourite photo of Jimmy in a Ferrari leans on the fireplace.
- Replayed the message my cousin sent me from a psychic so many times I can repeat all fifteen minutes of it by heart.
- Became irrationally angry when I've read quotes about death

saying shit like, 'What is grief if not love persevering?'
- Hidden a geocache in his honour at his favourite place so that random people get to read about him when they find it.
- Started feeling okay about it all.

Moving through losing

Swim in other people's memories of them. Over and over again. Over the years. Over time. Time and time again. Make sure you offer them your stories in return. Write them down in your Notes app and open them up on quiet nights when you're trying to get home. On the Hard Days, walk slowly down the street in sunglasses. Blame hayfever. Blame the election. Blame the war. Blame anything you want – people love a wreck. Be a wreck. Then pull yourself together – you can't live like this forever. Make physical places where their spirit can live. Believe in spirits. Believe in ghosts. Believe in signs. Believe in anything you want to get you through. But do more than just getting through; remember, you're down here, on earth. Make traditions, however strange they seem. Don't blame people who don't understand. Lucky people never really get it. Not fully. It's not their fault, they're just lucky. Watch the things they used to love. Open old books where they used to write. Trace their handwriting with your fingers, and feel both close and then very far away from them at the same time. Marvel and wrestle with time, and then let it (over time) relax within you. Go far away to places they never could. Get drunk in bars in foreign cities with strangers and tell them all about it. Feel both extremely happy and sad at the same time, but toast to what you got to have. Toast to what you've lost. Toast to keeping on living. Do it for them. And then, over and over again, each day, do it for yourself.

CHAPTER 5

Phoenixing

Phoenixing (verb): The phase that comes after everything burns down, and life as you know it feels like it'll never be good again, when you enter the most powerful flight of your life. The bad times are the ashes, and you are the bird.

Did the best I could and somehow I've ended up here
By Lucy and Bel

What they don't teach you in school is that there will be moments in your life when your whole sense of being burns to the ground. They teach you about trigonometry and STDs and war poetry. If you're lucky enough to still be listening, they teach you about DNA structures, how parliament works and the benefits of quantitative easing. But they don't tell you about the life-shattering moments that press up against every element of who you are and make you question what it means to be alive in the first place. They're not there to open the curtains on the weeks when you can't leave your room or get dressed. In the bleak days and the down times. During the months your friends will need to spend messaging you just to help you get through the day.

They don't tell you what it's like to fail in a desperate, irrevocable, unimaginable way. To be hurt by the world in a way you never thought possible. To drive down roads and not be able to turn back. And they definitely don't teach you what to do when your life inevitably breaks, and all you're left with are its pieces to slowly, painstakingly put back together again. If we were indie singer-songwriters, we'd make a song about this called 'Kintsugi'.

But what comes from these life-altering moments, the ones we, at the time, can't fathom getting out of, is one of life's ultimate gifts: phoenixing.

Out of the bleak, impossible fire of breaking down, breaking up or breaking into pieces, rises the biggest chance you get to leave the old version of who you thought you were behind and morph into something and someone you could never have imagined. When it comes, you have to take it.

When phoenixing happens, you can do anything you want. You can turn into a morning person. You can leave the party before it gets good. You can rebrand as someone who experiments with microdosing or joining a noise band. You can get a pixie crop. Sell all your clothes. Give live tarot readings on the internet. Start experimenting with parkour. You can do anything you need in the months that follow, and no one can judge you because your life has turned to ash and, until it increases in value, nothing is off-limits. Despite being incredibly bleak, this is an incredibly freeing feeling.

But it's difficult to see it that way when you're down at the bottom of a well. It's dark down there and, often, what you're turning to in those sharp, alone moments is a screen filled with people who're busy doing life perfectly. Or if they are admitting to being in a mess, it's often to the tune of a rediscovered Velvet Underground song, wrapped in a sage-coloured woven-bamboo duvet with a stick of Japanese incense burning in the background. Life has lost its ability to be a mess because that's difficult to film and make cute. We need to let it be ugly and offline for a while so it can come full force again.

If only we had known from the beginning that everything terrible eventually turns into something good, but only if we learn how to make sense of it. It seems as though the moments in life that are so dizzyingly good never last long enough, and the ones that crush you into someone unrecognisable feel as though they'll last forever. But through it all and out the other end? You take flight. You phoenix.

But first, you have to break.

Saving this for the next time
I Titanic

BEL: You know how I know you're phoenixing

                                      LUCY: how? (am i gonna cringe?)

BEL: This sounds super gushy
Like
You're gonna hate it
So sentimental

                                                  LUCY: omg
                                                             ok

BEL: I'm saying this because you need to hear it
It's your laugh
I can hear you laughing coming out of the podcast studio and
I know
Everything's kind of . . . shining around you

Not a sliver of an Evanescence 'wake me up inside' vibe[7] about you
Things are good again <3
I'm sounding like your husband on valentine's day or something

    LUCY: wanna know how i can tell you're phoenixing?

BEL: Only if you're not just making it up to pass on your discomfort

    LUCY: SHUT UP and let me tell you
ok usually it's when you're anywhere BUT the office (sorry)
you're up at all hours of the night tagging me in docs
and sending words (and as far as I can tell it's not insomnia induced)
and I espesh know you're phoenixing when you don't get
mad at me for roasting you on the mic about not knowing
some niche gen z thing
you take it in your stride
and when you play drums in our band
phoenixing energy

BEL: No, stop, you'll make me cry
Why has this turned into a two-part wedding speech

---

7 Evanescencing: The feeling of being in an intolerable moment and wanting it to be over quickly, so you can escape somewhere better. Made in reference to the hit 2003 song 'Bring Me To Life' by nu metal band Evanescence.

LUCY: is this what people in long termys get every day

BEL: Hmm. Def not when I was in a long termy
Maybe others
Maybe true love
Or maybe, I think it's just what you notice if you've gone down and come back up, you know

LUCY: brb just filing these messages away for next time
I titanic[8]

---

8 Titanicing: The feeling of slowly nose-diving into a period of extreme disaster, fatigue or hunger.

GOING DOWN WITH THIS SHIP (AND COMING BACK UP AGAIN)

FADE IN:

INT. APARTMENT - MORNING.

GIRL, late twenties, sits on the floor of her apartment in her underwear, a selection of nail polish bottles arranged around her. She's noticeably gaunt, her hair in a greasy bird's nest on top of her head. A stack of cardboard boxes sits in the far corner. The morning light streams in. FRIEND is on speakerphone.

                  GIRL
              (dramatically)
  What if I'm alone forever?

Cut to the kitchen bench, strewn with dirty wine glasses and plates, keys, tampons: girl mess.

                 FRIEND
  Well, what if I die tomorrow?

GIRL

What if I get on *The Amazing Race* and get eliminated in the first episode?

FRIEND

Exactly. We're all just living in fragile chaos. What have you been doing when we leave at night?

A rubbish truck drives past, and glass bottles smash as they're tipped into it.

GIRL

That sound's a metaphor for my life, by the way. I'm like. . . that Dido album — *Life For Rent*.

Girl lies down in exasperation on her living room floor. We see her half-empty bookshelf and pictures missing from their hooks on the wall.

FRIEND
(laughing)
Shut up. What have you been doing alone at night?

GIRL
(closing her eyes as if confessing)
Drinking. . . a bit more chardonnay. And then dancing to ABBA until I lose my breath and have to go to sleep.

> FRIEND

Exactly.

> GIRL
> (sitting back up)

Exactly what?

We hear FRIEND'S coffee grinder whir briefly in the background.

> FRIEND
> (animated)

You have all this time back. You get to. . . I don't know, be a girl again? Figure out what you want. You get to, like, step out of an airport terminal and decide who you want to be. Love is lovely, and I love that I'm in it, but also, babe, it's not everything.

> GIRL

Can you tell me this every time I speak to you until it becomes like an insufferable Carrie Bradshaw montage?

> FRIEND

Of course. Because I love you. Now wash your hair, eat something substantial and go outside.

END.

The heart is heaven, the heart is hell
By Bel

I need to acknowledge how cliché it feels to begin talking about phoenixing from a breakup and the deep sensation that your entire life, as you know it, has been absolutely obliterated. It's a real, 21st century, Bechdel test failure. And yet, here we are. When I read back over my journal from that time, when I was 29 and breaking up with who I thought was the love of my life, I sound barely alive. I'm a skinny, numb wreck driving around listening to the same four Lana Del Rey songs on repeat ('When's it gonna be my tuuuuuuuurn???'), furiously vaping because it's something to do with my breath and something to do other than talk about it. I'm religiously hanging out with my female friends as though it's my last night on earth, and have never experienced so much silence in my life. I hate a cliché feeling because I think I've watched enough YouTube tutorials to be better than this.

I have to start this on the floor so that you believe that I've been to some type of bottom, so you trust me when I say I know what utter personal destruction feels like. We'd been together for two years, and living with someone felt like the greatest act of adulthood I had ever undertaken. I'd chased men around the world, caught trains, video chatted over time zones – even bent my body to fit into shapes I thought they wanted. But physically building a life with someone felt like the triumphant and sacred pinnacle of what a successful woman could do, and finally laid to rest all the worried glances I'd get at weddings or turning up to another dinner alone. The fallout of this ending was completely and utterly eviscerating, and I'm ashamed to say I took it as a personal failure because I'd been the girl enjoying sitting on aeroplanes and in waiting rooms next to someone, smiling away as though *that was my life now*. Being That Girl is so fun because you feel accomplished and you always have someone to do something with on your birthday and come home to on a Friday night. It seemed insane to me at the time, that I could manage a meeting, pitch a million-dollar campaign, stay up late SHE-EOing my way through a presentation, but I could not fulfil one of the most basic aspects of life: keeping someone in love with me.

This is where we cut back to the opening scene. There's something so unimaginably humiliating about standing in a pile of someone's things that you know as intimately as you know the story of how they got there in the first place and that they're are now no longer relevant to your life, except for the way they'll become artefacts in the story you tell of it. You're holding an internet router and wondering who's going to have to go on hold with the provider, to eventually stop hearing 'April Sun in Cuba' on repeat, only to tell them that no, living together didn't work out and could they please close down your account without asking any more questions. Or who will be responsible for sending out all the press releases telling people you've failed and won't be coming to the thing together. Or what you will tell your parents.

In the movies, failures are for middle-aged men whose businesses collapse in a stock market crash or who cheat on their wives when they become enlisted as spies but fail at that, too. I'd done everything I could: read Alain de Botton's books on love, gone about it slowly, been honest, been to therapy, had my own interests, given thoughtful gifts, remembered birthdays, made spontaneous plans, cooked breakfast for his friends and yet all of that wasn't enough. The realisation that you can do everything in your control and things will still not work out is one of the hardest lessons to fully arrive at and accept while you lie awake at night grieving a future you thought you were promised but never got to have. It's very levelling to learn that not even you, no matter how hard you try and how many carbon credits you offset, are protected from change.

'Where's that bloke of yours?' the guy on the bottom floor of our apartment block asks as I'm struggling to carry another banana box up the stairwell. He told me on the day we moved in that he bought gold jewellery, melted it down and sold it for a living.

'Oh, um, we're not together anymore,' I reply, trying to look as though something really important (my entire life falling to pieces) is happening upstairs and urgently needs my attention.

'What?! No! That's such a shame. I really thought you'd be together forever,' he said, standing in his cluttered entranceway. 'I even said to one of my mates – those gold dealers I was telling you about – to keep an eye out if he ever had, you know, a ring in mind,' he says with a smile. (Why are you smiling? Literally why).

'Thank you, that was very thoughtful.' I'm moving up the stairs and hoping I'll never have to see him again.

'Such a shame.'

I shut the front door and have a good cry. Minutes later, Johanna shows up in her pyjamas having just ordered more Vietnamese to my door. 'I just thought the worst thing a friend can do is turn up to a freshly snapped heart looking snatched as fuck. I'm hungover.

And you look like a tiny bird. We need to eat. And then you need to tell me everything that's happened, and then I need to tell you that as I was driving here, I realised I don't think I could pick that man out in a lineup of criminals, and if that doesn't say everything you need to hear, I don't know what does.'

'I feel like such a failure,' I say.

'Who cares? Your life's about to change, babe. In the best way.'

God bless the friendships that can wrench you out of delusion.

During this time living like a fucking meme, I met Luce. Soon after, I started writing for SYSCA, and small, precious parts of myself very slowly started returning. As the months amassed in that annoying way everyone always says they do, my life started to take flight again. Luce and I began meeting in the early hours of the morning before work, in the café round the corner from our office, talking and planning and laughing about all our audacious dreams, wondering if one day they would come true.

Dreaming. That's where phoenixing comes from.

In the absence of being brought coffee in bed, like in a Frank O'Hara poem, and parents visiting, and other normcore couple admin, like upgrading our toothbrushes, I had all this time back to dream. I had weeknights. Weekends. Sunday mornings. Slivers of time to read books and voice message my friends and come home and just . . . flick through a magazine. In between the times when I wasn't spiralling and lying on my apartment floor, I had the rocks by the sea to lie on with my friends and relay travel stories of the girls we used to be. I had hours on my balcony with them unpacking our careers, booking campsites, getting drunk on pink pitchers of homemade cosmopolitans, selling old clothes online, ratting out ex-crushes and other romantic disappointments. Everyone always talks about time as the great healer when you're heartbroken, but it's more than that: time becomes a beautiful chasm that opens up and reconnects you with your strange and singular self. It lets you go away and make your own secrets at a time when all you have is questions.

In among the disappointment of what was categorically meant to be the loneliest time of my life, I became the most alive I'd ever been. Down there in the ashes of realising the person I had chosen was not the person I needed, I found what I'd lost along the way: who I wanted to be.

When I think back on that life-burning-to-the-ground heartbreak, which I hope will be my last but who's to ever truly know or say, I want to kneel down on the floor next to that one-winged pigeon who was once me and promise her with every bone in my body that the unthinkable will happen: things will change. Life will put itself back together. You will fly again.

What phoenixing feels like
By Lucy

Phoenixing feels like making plans and keeping them.
Phoenixing feels like laughing with your whole chest.
Phoenixing feels like when you want to sing in the car again.
Phoenixing feels like hauling all the clothes that remind you of the hard times into the donation bin.
Phoenixing feels like betting on yourself.
Phoenixing feels like falling asleep without having to put on a podcast or a rerun of that TV show you watched when you were 16.
Phoenixing feels like wearing colour because you aren't afraid to be seen.
Phoenixing feels like picking up the phone to your best friend when they call.
Phoenixing feels like not lying about how you are.
Phoenixing feels like the day your Citalopram stops making you feel nauseous.
Phoenixing feels like saying yes to meeting your friends instead of finding a way to cancel on them.
Phoenixing feels like one small good thing happening, and then another, and then another.
Phoenixing feels like taking a risk.

Phoenixing feels like believing you're worth more.

Phoenixing feels like dusting the cobwebs off your guitar.

Phoenixing feels like there's magic in the world again, or at least in you.

Phoenixing feels like being open to spontaneity because you're not scared of the repercussions.

Phoenixing feels like letting joy have its moment.

Phoenixing feels like demanding to be seen.

Phoenixing feels like thinking about things that are not to do with yourself for once.

Phoenixing feels like the bravery you've been missing.

Phoenixing feels both a lot like your old self and nothing like them at all.

Phoenixing feels like you deserve it.

Phoenixing won't always come at you as some huge revelation. Sometimes it will just lay with you, tucked under the covers until you're ready to notice it. Just you wait.

Living well is the best revenge
By Bel

Another ad agency, 2016

I'm 23 when I land in Australia from surfing around Sri Lanka and start working at another ad agency. It's a small indie run by men who seemed constantly on the cusp of both becoming famous and the company having to close down. I'm the first person in my family to graduate university, have a student loan or work in a corporate job. All those firsts stacked up like a glass trophy I'm terrified of dropping. I would rather work myself into oblivion than admit defeat. And the danger that comes with this mindset is if you let the visions of who you think you need to be and the responsibilities that come with that persona envelop you, you can very easily trade your self-worth for what someone can get away with. But this was 2016, and we were still drinking from takeaway cups with wild abandon and hiring influencers to take Boomerang videos with product placements.

The work is exhilarating. There are drinks every day after work. Everyone wears sneakers. The office is actually an apartment building. For the first time in my life, I'd found myself in the all-consuming tailspin of falling in love with a new city, a new identity and an office full of people who knew nothing about me except that after five wines I'd make them play Dave Dobbyn's 'Slice of Heaven' on repeat so often, they nicknamed me 'Dobbs'. This was the sports team I never made it into in high school, but even better because I got paid to be there. Plus, women were now allowed to wear sneakers to work, so I could walk to work from my apartment and not get shin splints along the way.

On my first day, I was given a pencil, a desktop computer and three months to prove I was worth my salary. 'You know how it is,' the agency founder in new double-monk shoes and a cap says to me with a smile, 'that indie, relentless hustle.' 'The hustle' seems like the coolest concept I've heard in my life, because if you pull it off, you've really made it, you know. I have $42,000 of student debt and I'm desperate to prove that I can do this and my degree was all worth it. The guy managing me cannot relate. We cannot relate on any level. Except for the time he mentioned spending a weekend away on a luxury farm escape (and I could mention my knowledge of sheep drench and farm whistles), which I remember being called Killarney, but in hindsight, I realise that's just the name of the farm they were always trying to save in, *McLeod's Daughters*, the Australian drama about a group of woman running a farm that I was obsessed with in high school. He loomed over me when we stood up to present at meetings and this is where I learned how to overcompensate for how small you can be made to feel.

Working in advertising has this TV-style effect on you. It lets you believe that the industry is the centre of the world, and it's so thrilling and self-important. There's money and lunches and late nights being offered drugs in back rooms and dancing, as though no one's paying for anything. Working in advertising overseas was a whole new level because everything was bigger and shinier and had a greater possibility of 'making' me. I was older now, and had a surer sense of myself and what I was worth. Or so I thought. What follows broke me into a thousand pieces.

Work gets intense, fast, often accumulating into 50-, 60-, sometimes 80-hour weeks, making up advertising pitch-decks for brands who want to be like Nike but can't afford to. Very early on, a famous advertising director tells me working 'here' (he points around, referring to the industry, I guess) is like taking meth. 'It stretches you so far, it's hard to go back to normal! Ha ha ha.' He's just won a trophy cabinet of awards for a campaign that was entered into every category. 'But the highs – the highs are worth it!' he says, pats me on the back and walks off into the crowd after seeing someone famous to talk to.

I start breaking out in hives. Getting sick all the time. Cancelling on friends at the last minute. I stay later and later at work, eating an orange for dinner at my desk and stop texting anyone back. It's the early Girlboss era, everyone has their work apps on their phone, and no one thinks it's insane to be emailing about advertising copy version_9 from the supermarket aisle at 10 o'clock at night. TikToks about doing the bare minimum and having boundaries at work will come later, but for now we're all living in the endless ambition delusion. Women had all this new opportunity laid out for us and the worst thing we could possibly do was to waste it being all emotional about it at work. I'm young and lucky by a lot of standards, and I have nothing to complain about. I have to do better, I think, but better never ends.

Bad things keep happening, and I continue to ignore them because there's nothing worse than being an hysterical woman. The more messed up it gets, the more determined I am to not make a big deal of it in the way hysterical women do. It gets so bad that at one point, I throw up in the bathroom, wipe my mouth with the back of my hand and walk straight into another pitch meeting.

Work is the ultimate collision of our internal worlds (what we know, how much we think that's worth) and our external needs (the money we need in order to survive), which makes it so hard to know what's right, what's enough and when to stop. I'm embarrassed and determined, and things get worse. I get kicked out of a meeting once my more attractive workmate returns from her lunch break. At a leaving drinks, a client reveals a guy on my projects had told her I was just his intern. When I finally work up the courage to confront him, he denies everything and leaves a chocolate brownie on my desk the next morning. *Am I making this all up?* I stay later and work harder, desperate to prove myself.

You have to understand these are the days before 'gaslighting' entered our lexicon, when it was still a vague reference to that 1930s play about the man who plays with the gas lamps in his house to fool his wife into thinking she's going crazy. But when someone starts to mess with your perception of reality, you start to question your own truths and believe theirs instead. Maybe I did write those numbers wrong. Maybe I shouldn't speak in the meeting. Maybe this is just what work is. Maybe I should be here until 9pm every night. Maybe I'm making a big deal out of nothing. Maybe this is all my fault. I make a complaint to management and they recommend taking a public speaking course so I seem more confident to clients.

Work is not a competition of endurance. It should not ever be about who can stay up and send their emails the latest or reply the fastest. When we strip work of its humanity, it strips us of ours. We get reduced to money-making things without real lives outside our working hours, as opposed to people who go to work in order to make a living, and then come home to the people and things that make them real. I know this now, and we are coming to know this more as a society. But I didn't know it then, because I was young and because I thought that if work wasn't working, it was somehow my fault, and not the system I was working within.

Something physical is going on. I get so desperate for confirmation that I start seeing a holistic doctor. The fortnightly ritual goes like this: early in the morning I catch an Uber across the city, swipe my credit card for $350 per session, he runs tests, pricks me with needles, fills a tote bag up with supplements and puts me on a vitamin drip before sending me on my way. I sit in his tiny white room reading old magazines about Princess Diana while he infuses me with nutrients that my body's stopped being able to make. Most mornings there are spent biting back tears and flicking pages, reading about revenge dresses and the impeccable art of looking chic at an AIDS hospital to distract myself from what's going on. This romantic young woman everyone loved, but no one took seriously, and look what happened to her? It's hard not to get existential in there, drawing ridiculous parallels between my working life and one of the most famously scorned women in the world. Diana and I become friends. The ordeal at the doctor's takes an hour, and then I'm patched up and back in time for the day's first meeting. It becomes a gruelling, cash-haemorrhaging, secret struggle I have with my body and my mind, and I've never felt so alone in my life.

Two months of shuttling back and forth across the city in peak-hour traffic and draining my savings, and nothing's changing. I'm still sick all the time, still vomiting at work and still taking the entire weekend to recover only to do it all again. I lose weight and the colour in my face. Sometimes I get dressed to go to work and just sit on the end of my bed for long stretches of time, completely unable to move. At one point, someone mentions a life-changing witch they once saw when their life was crumbling, so I catch the tram out to see her. She's dressed in purple psychedelic clothing in a hot room, and after our session, she delivers a 10-litre tank of 'magic water' to my office. She's cast a spell and no one else is to drink it. The tank takes up half my desk space. I run out of stories to explain what it's doing there, and everyone wants a sip. At an impromptu office party, we use it as a 'magic mixer', and everyone thinks they're capable of anything.

The next morning at the doctor, things come undone.

'Bel, your tests have come back showing no change again,' the doctor pulls his computer chair closer towards me. I've spent so much time in this room by now, I feel like I know everything about him: where he trained, his children's names and what his wife wore on holiday to Fiji in 2003. In return, he knows the inner workings of my failing body. My aches. He knows about the people I work with, my friends at pubs and, most importantly, my love for the sartorial collection and wider significance of Lady Di. I wonder if we are friends and, if I died, whether he would come to my funeral out of more than social obligation. 'I've never seen anything like this. You're on the highest dose of everything I can give you, and nothing is changing. It's like you have the body of a 65-year-old who hasn't had a day off in their life. You have Chronic Fatigue Syndrome'. My body goes numb, and I can't stop the hot sting of tears; I make sharp breathy gasps the way Manic Pixie Dream Girl characters do in movies.

'I just. Am doing. Everything I can,' I say in gulps, crushing a cheap tissue and digging my nails into my hand.

'I'm sorry, Bel, but it's not working. You need to stop working.

Things are never going to get better if you keep doing the same thing.' I wonder if he would write that down for me in an email that I can forward to my boss, then slip out the back door of the office never to be seen again.

It's incredible how the universe serves you. At that moment, all I can feel is the sweat on my palms, the lino on the floor, and an overwhelming appreciation for the doctor and all he's done for me. This was never going to work, and if I ignored all the signs, it would get seriously worse. I have no choices left. I hand in my resignation in a meeting with my bosses where I can't stop crying. That evening, I get an email from the someone higher up in the company inviting me to breakfast the next morning. I do what I've always done for work except for the days when it was impossible to leave the house: I wake up, I pull on my kitten-heeled boots and I show up.

We meet in a café that serves coffee in mason jars. He looks like the lead talent in a life-insurance ad, and I wonder whether he has ever paid capital gains tax or, more importantly, whether he knows anything about me. We say hello and order quickly. One thing about successful businessmen is that they don't waste time. This is probably because they wrote that saying 'time is money', so every minute they're spending on you, they're missing out on making more money somewhere else.

'Let me cut straight to it,' he says as he moves the morning's newspaper to the corner of the table. 'You're young and working at an agency that's about to go big time, and you won't, I promise, ever get an opportunity like this again. If you go, you'll regret it for the rest of your life.' The waiter arrives with our coffees and sets them down in front of us

The room goes fuzzy, and I can't hear anything, like when you're about to faint or as an aeroplane's taking off. I start Evanescencing,[9] thinking 'wake me up, wake me up inside', and want to teleport anywhere in the world but here. This man who'd made millions from TV commercials in the 1980s (1970s?) in faded chinos and a grey t-shirt was now stepping in to tell me how to stop ruining my life. He's talking about how lucky I am to have a chance taken on me in the first place and that most young women would die for an opportunity like this. And what was I going to do now, anyway?

I stop listening. He doesn't notice as the whole year flashes in front of me: getting to work and rushing to the downstairs bathroom in cold sweats. Getting home at 10pm on a Wednesday night, so exhausted I could only summon the energy to eat a chopped-up cucumber with cheese on my bedroom floor. The parties. The pitches. The witch I'd gone to see and her supposedly healing water. The numbers in my documents changing. Being sent passive aggressive texts under the table while in client meetings. Uncontrollably crying in front of management about what was happening, desperately saying, 'Please – I'm not making this up.' I've officially been Lemonied.[10]

I think of the helicopters and the celebrities and the sunglasses I'd bought to wear to the parties on yachts. Of the complaints I'd made. The silences I'd been met with. The hours spent sweating through my polyester outfits, trying to be taken seriously. Everything I'd been complicit in along the way. I put my cup down. I say thank you and goodbye. I get on a tram. I get back to my apartment and

---

9 See page 167.
10 Lemonied: An affectionate reference to author Lemony Snicket's *A Series of Unfortunate Events* books, used to refer to when bad things keep happening to you, one after the other.

book a flight home. At that moment, I choose losing. I'd already lost everything about who I thought I was. There was nothing else left.

To admit that where you've ended up is the wrong place, that you've failed catastrophically and also been failed by life is to admit there's magic in the world, and sometimes it's lost on you. That there's always darkness at play, no matter how hard we try to keep it at bay or remain immune. I'd glorified work so much, but at what cost? What is the cost of working when it erodes our ability to live? I was disappointed the answers to these questions did not lie in the bottom of the witch's water tank lying on my desk.

I return to my hometown and speak to no one. I say I'll go back to my job and then email them in a night panic, reneging on my promises. I lie in bed with the curtains drawn while my mum pokes small plates of food through the door, lost for words while I hit play on another episode of *Dawson's Creek*. My eyes are red; I can't lift my head, wear my clothes or speak to anyone. I'm an empty ship out at sea, and no one can predict the weather.

The worst part about it is when I begin to realise I should have stood up for myself more. I should have trusted myself enough to know what was too wrong to tolerate, to know that I should have left the job months earlier. But when you're young, you're so vulnerable to what other people see for you, what they want out of their own lives and how their ambitions can eclipse your own welfare. I wish I'd believed my intuition more and I wish I'd believed in my own objective sense of truth – that when your body breaks, it's often the final straw and a sign of something much greater at play. Friends who saw me while I had that job, shepherding my body across the city to meet them (always late) for drinks (always too many) describe watching the slow decline of someone they loved as painful to watch. 'It's like you were in an abusive relationship,' my friend Simon once remarked. When you think of it, the way we work and love aren't that different.

Being at home is difficult. I have no compass, and my parents are kind and worried and busy working their own honest jobs and living by the seasons. I'm like a teenager again, lying on the floor listening to the back catalogue of The Postal Service and other hits from *The O.C.* that speak to me like nothing else ever could. After a month of living like this, almost exclusively wearing a grey marl tracksuit in my parents' spare room and living on a diet of beige food, I slowly start to get better. I go on walks that get slightly longer each day – to the bridge, to the next fence post, to the river's edge. I start to answer calls from my friends, whose care in a crisis has never ceased to amaze me. A creative director I'd befriended gives my email to a career coach who owes him a favour and we arrange a video call.

Jo has statement glasses and a shelf of Ottolenghi cookbooks in the background of her video call. I tell her everything. We speak for two hours and, finally, the insanity of what happened properly collides with reality. 'OK, this is what you need to do. You need to go on a long walk and think about the experiences you want to bring forward and those you want to leave behind forever,' she says. I'm trying to glean more details of her put-together Melbourne home, where I suspect she owns linen aprons and hosts a lot of dinner parties with her well-adjusted group of diverse friends. It's encouraging to know such a life is possible even though I can't imagine it for myself. I also can't believe I'm actually talking to a career coach. I think I'd like to maybe get a tattoo and start teaching yoga after this.

'And then?' I ask. I cannot see a world after this 'walk,' although I can now make it to the bridge and back, let alone a life.

'Then you go and create your poetic existence. One piece at a time. You put all that energy into relentlessly pursuing the life you so deeply deserve. It won't work out how you think and it won't ever be perfect. But you don't stop.' This is the first moment in the burned-down haze where I feel the faintest spark that something good could have actually come from this.

'And before we go, I just want to tell you something I don't want you to ever forget.'

'What's that?' I ask. This is the point where I wonder if what she was going to say would be so poignant I would consider it for the basis of a new tattoo, maybe in Latin.

'Living well is the best revenge. Whenever things get hard, or your plans feel like they're running away from you, you must always remember this.'

I didn't need a purple psychic tapping a wand onto a 10-litre container of water to validate my feelings. I didn't need a fellow burned-out woman at a corporate event telling me to make a vision board. I didn't need to stream a panel discussion on how to negotiate my worth or a blog post teaching me to hover my mouth open when men talk over me at work so they realise what they're doing. I needed to believe that deep down, I was always worth protecting and that work shouldn't come at such a cost. I had also realised, over the course of that destruction, that the more consumed I was by my job, the less interesting I became outside of it. We want these realisations to come so fast, like everything else in our lives, but more often they're slow revelations that happen over time and begin to crystallise just as we need them most.

It's getting dark. I shut my laptop, pull the curtains open and pad out to sit on the edge of my parents' deck so my feet touch the rough grass. Everything has changed so unfathomably. I am so far from where I wanted to be and right back where I'd started. I close my body very tight in on itself and vow that I'll never let anyone take that power away from me again. And to stop marketing beer brands to men in linen shirts. They can do that themselves.

How to phoenix

Let yourself break. Be both graceful and violent about it. Wear ugly clothes and listen to Dido on your bedroom floor, but don't stay down there so long that melancholy becomes your defining feature. Find someone who's been through either the same or worse than you, and talk to them often. Avoid Lucky People because they won't understand. Sit in the sun where no one can see you and lose track of time. Keep company with people who tell you truths that escalate in meaning as you get better. Move slowly. Ignore the internet. Write down your dumb feelings each day in a small notebook you keep under your bed, and watch them change. Mute people from high school posting in front of SOLD signs. Say no to social obligations. Let people bring you treats, sit on the end of your bed and feel sorry for you. Draw the curtains. Open the windows. Rearrange your room. Get rid of your old clothes like a snake shedding its skin. Mark each day with a number out of ten and watch the number slowly get better. If it doesn't, ask for help. Find a TV show with seven seasons so that by the end of it, you're so sick of the main character's drama, you realise your life has changed more than theirs. Steal flowers from strangers' fencelines and put them in a small vase next to your bed. Watch them wilt. Do it again. Hang out with rich people and see that you can own boats and still have problems. Ignore your friend's mum, who says she has never seen you like this. Turn off the car and sit in there for a while. Pretend the person who hurt you has died. Find help in places you've never been before. Avoid the supermarket where you grew up. Put a monthly reminder in your calendar to reward yourself for getting through. Listen to every second person who'll say to you, 'Time will change this,' but know it's more complicated than that. Other people and certain things will help – but it's you who will save your own life. Just watch.

CHAPTER 6

On falling in love (or not)

And not losing the romantic will to live.

God, it's brutal out here
By Lucy and Bel

What if another heartbreak literally kills me? What if I don't want romance at all? What if I want it so bad, but it never comes, and I catch a sickness one day and die alone in my apartment because all my friends and family think I've just put my phone on Do Not Disturb? Why am I at another hens party? Will this ever happen to me? Do I want it to? If one more person ghosts me, can I take a romantic sabbatical[11] but never return?

Love has been marketed to us our whole lives as a milestone achievement; one that, should you not reach it by a particular age, means you've missed a boat everyone else has caught, leaving you wondering whether it will ever return to pick you up. Someone made up these timelines (meet someone in your twenties, share a bedroom, go on holidays, take photos across the table, meet the love of your life, buy a dog and settle down in your thirties), and even though we know they're arbitrary, that doesn't stave off annoying relatives asking if we've 'settled down with someone good yet'. Love is divine and dizzy and delicious and lucky and powerful and

---

11 Romantic sabbatical: To take time out of the dating game to focus on fulfilment through your own life and take a break from composing chill yet engaging text messages to potential trysts.

insane, but its timing in our lives forces us to confront the fact that some things are uncontrollable, no matter how hard we try. It's so annoying like that. The experience of modern romance for women is the ultimate collision of what the patriarchy's held us back from and what technology enables. It's on our phones, in the palms of our hands. It's both readily available (swipe) and ephemeral (ghosting). It's both fun (crushing and making out and fate) and a logistical nightmare (2am texts reading 'U up?'). It's always been a game, but it's now more complicated than ever. Now the secret's out that women can work, and you have to pay them the same as men, our need for love is less economical. Less dependent. But most of us want it just the same. We still need romantic love, but now we need to learn it's not everything.

In advertising, people who're single with no dependents are called 'SINKs' (Single Income, No Kids); we both joke about it all the time:

Just going home now to SINK.

SINK into the sofa and watch whatever I like and not have to tend to anyone else's life.

SINK into my dwindling bank account and eat toast for dinner because I don't need to cook for anyone but myself.

SINK into my solitude.

SINK into a soft pant.

SINK another bottle of red.

SINK into a book and not look up till it's past midnight.

Solitude can be wonderfully self-indulgent if we let it. And other times, when you're wrestling a set of drawers you've bought from Facebook Marketplace into the back of an Uber, you feel like the lead character in a mockumentary about being alone. (Will she make it up the stairs? What will she make for dinner? Will anyone help her zip the back of her dress up in time?!) We can't always control our circumstances, but we can choose to reframe the stories we tell ourselves when we're in our own company.

What follows are the stories of two opposites; someone in their mid-twenties who's never fallen in love, and the other in their early thirties, believing in romance despite its gamified modern reality.

Love is real. Love is fun. Love is everything good and hard and valuable. Romantic love is not the only love. Love is at the centre of how we feel about everything, especially ourselves and what we think we deserve.

When you've never been in love
By Lucy

What is it they say about a woman alone? She's got a few cats, a vibrator or two in her beside table and she's miserable. She's too free-spirited to hold down a relationship or too obsessed with climbing the corporate ladder to find the time, and she's sitting at home on Saturday nights yearning. Has she tried lowering her expectations? Tried going to therapy? Has she tried the apps?

I've never been in proper love, and let me tell you: me and my sinful bedside table are just fine.

Do I need to reassure you here that I'm not a total spinster? I've had flings with people I've become best friends with, boyfriends who were around for a season and not exactly a reason, and people I've tried to love, maybe even should have loved, but couldn't. Therapists have asked me about the relationships I saw growing up, and I've told them that as a kid I never saw one that I'd want for myself. Instead, I saw couples who were indifferent to each other, who hated each other or who wanted to leave but being alone seemed a fear too big to face. At best, I saw the type of relationship you have with the jeans that stopped fitting you four years ago but that you hold onto anyway, hoping one day they'll fit like they used to again. It could be that these couples all just got married too young and that they were products of the age they grew up in, where you met at a pub, connected over a phone line, got married and popped out a few kids who soon become the only thing you had in common. I'm sure relationships are different these days; I'm just not sure I want one. Sue me!

Am I doing my twenties wrong though?

We're told that in your twenties, you're supposed to be out all the time, being distracted by dates and anniversaries, disappointments and star-crossed lovers. I love nothing more than helping my friends navigate all of that. We've always been different – they're on apps where you swipe to find someone you might be moderately compatible with, I'm on apps burning auto-captions on videos. They're going out to chic wine bars and meeting people who talk about fishing and *Pulp Fiction*. I'm going out to chic wine bars and meeting people who want to help me migrate to the best newsletter platform for a small-scale start-up. Different strokes for different folks I guess.

Maybe this is just how I justify my intermittent loneliness, but looking back at my proudest moments, I can't help but wonder if they would have happened if I had been busy being in love. If I had had a partner when I was bored in that lecture theatre, would SYSCA exist, or would I have texted them and asked if they wanted to go and get ramen for dinner? If I hadn't spent all my free time over those next few years sharing parts of myself online or responding to DMs, emails and comments, would I have been on stage in New York talking to people from *The New York Times* or *The Atlantic* about the platform and community we'd built at SYSCA, giving those publications tips for how they could do the same? If

I was off having brunch with my 'better half' every Sunday morning instead of catching up on emails and world events, would I be getting brunch with my idols today? I know some people choose both: I'm just not one of them. I was intoxicated by freedom, knowing that if I wanted to do something extraordinary I had to choose a different adventure. So I did.

Sunday mornings are for sex, loneliness or your passions

When you choose the latter, you're choosing yourself. Your friends might not get it. You'll catch yourself on another group holiday, in another designated single bed, spending another night listening to your couple friends ask each other if they'd like to 'get a few things and split them' for dinner. These moments make you think about the single tax and how your life is more expensive when you've got no one to split rent with and no wedding registry to furnish your home. How you'll attend expensive hens weekends at wineries and buy uncomfortable shoes to attend 'destination' weddings, knowing these may be sunk costs that your friends will never return. Your friends say things like, 'One day you're going to meet someone who changes the way you feel about all of this!' and they'll genuinely believe it. You'll humour them, and wake up early the next day to go and find a spot to write a newsletter or stay up late researching something for a podcast and thank God you didn't have anyone in bed beside you asking you to be quiet or turn down the brightness on your phone.

When your ambition takes the spot in the bed next to you, there are sacrifices. Of course there are. Do I feel like I'm left out of a secret club that you're only allowed into after you've posted something with a caption like: 'Three laps around the sun with this one!'? Sure I do. But I'm kinda obsessed with that for me. Your twenties might be about finding someone who loves you deeply, shows you the world and holds your hand because they want to. I'm obsessed with that for you.

I've heard love is a drug

Never being in love is how I imagine people might feel if they've never experimented with drugs – you don't know what you're missing, but you always wonder if your life might be fuller if you tried it. There is always wondering. What would it be like to relate to most of Taylor Swift's discography? To have someone to put your bags into the plane's overhead compartment? Would you understand poetry better? Would you care about Shakespeare more? Since you can't roll over and ask the love of your life, you have to ask yourself. The empty space beside you becomes filled with the businesswoman, the writer, the joke teller, the sibling, the friend, and all the other things you choose to be when you're not waiting for someone else to choose you. An empty space is not loneliness. It gives you room to build out your life. To let people come and go when they need to. To fill it with whatever you want, whenever you want. Plus, an empty space means no one is snoring.

When you've never received a good morning text or had someone to finish your sentences, you learn to have a good morning on your own and to write your own stories. You stop blaming the timing, the planets or bad luck and instead choose to focus on the little things that remind you that even without a lover, you are loved. There is love in every 'this reminded me of you' or 'text me when you get home' message you receive. There is love in every song you're sent or book you're recommended. There is love in everyone who listens to the things that excite you. There is love in the people who accompany you to the bathroom or help you move house or tell you they're proud of you when you're off chasing some new dream.

Even if you've never been *in* it, there is still love. The romance can come later, if you want.

Cheat codes for flying solo

No one promised you it would be this hard or easy, so just go with it. Life has a gap in it; everyone feels it. Do as little damage as possible to yourself trying to fill it. Don't get depressed by the everyday machinations of life, turn them into small accomplishments instead. Love yourself but not so much that people get the impression you think you're better than them. Chances are, you are. Leave the party whenever you want and laugh about it when you get home. Your mystery is your currency, give it away thoughtfully. Don't freak out if you feel lonely, but if you are lonely, go find out what's missing. Get a hobby. Book a trip. Fill the void, but move with intention and do it mindfully. Ask for what you want. Don't complain if you don't get it, try again in a different way. Have a good, light reason as to why you don't have another half when someone asks, and say, 'Ha ha!' at the end, so they know you're actually all good about it. Get good style so people know you're happy with who you are. Keep your jealousies to yourself – that's what everyone else is doing. Print off something inspirational and stick it to your mirror. Meet strangers, say 'Hi' through your eyelashes as though you have a secret and you know what you're doing with it. End up on the backs of their motorcycles flying through the warm night in the sole pursuit of red, hot joy. Take photos to remember details only you will notice. Document yourself and how you're changing. Keep your own secrets. Tell your own lies. Write down your unruly desires and don't show anyone else, but hold yourself accountable. See your life as yours and not in the shape of anyone else's. In the moments that aren't bright and worth bragging about, go back to working. Go back to building your life.

Date night

BEL: This just in
I will not be home tonight because
And not to make it all about men because that's so boring but
I have a date

                              LUCY: omg who
                                        i will be out
                  and then home bc i have a dinner and then
                      i have to race back and be on a zoom
                              with the white house lol

BEL: Omg
Is this a joke
Your life
Can't deal
Will Biden be there
What will you say to him

                                      LUCY: shut up
                       and no he won't but yes
                                      it's wild

BEL: I'm getting back out there
I'm doing it. I'm letting love in
I'm going on a second date with Organic Suit Guy

                LUCY: obsessed.
                where are you going

BEL: For dinner
Actually
Is that even safe?
Should I be doing this?
Maybe I should cancel. I'm cancelling

            LUCY: i think you should go
            wait have you looked him up online
            does he have creds

BEL: He has creds I read them on his LinkedIn profile
But who's to say what that even means these days

    LUCY: i'm going to put one of my airtags in your wallet
just so that if you don't come home i've got your real-time
                                location
            and so i can sleep knowing you're safe
                also send me his address

BEL: Ok sent

                      LUCY: gorge
              what are you gonna wear?

lol
jeans and a nice top?

BEL: I'm thinking
A simple dress and sneaker
Nothing intimidating
Nothing OTT
Watermelon colour combo (naturally)
What could possibly go wrong

LUCY: let love in katherine heigl
i'll be on the other end of the airtag if u need me

BEL: Kathy Heigl like 27 Dresses? I die a thousand deaths

LUCY: HAHAHA
be safe and just go and fucking have fun

BEL: I will!
I mean, I'll try!
And I'll be sure to phone the White House should anything untoward unfold

I'd like to be in love, but I'm busy being here, on a date with you
By Bel

I'm thinking about whether I should text you what I'm wearing just in case you don't recognise me and we have one of those awful who-the-hell-are-yous outside the restaurant. I'm thinking this as I'm walking to the low-stakes location I'll definitely never go back to, thinking about all the other things I could be doing this evening. Like going to a ceramics class, or cooking dinner so I'll have a Tupperware lunch tomorrow, or watching movie trailers on YouTube until 11:30pm, or lying on my best friend's living room floor with blackhead strips on, ignoring my notifications. I'm thinking I hope this spritz of my perfume is worth the expense of using it tonight. I estimate it to cost $0.75 per spray. I think about Return On Investment.

We're both sitting down now and I'm thinking, you're alright. Like, not incredible, but alright. All the advice says to keep going if you feel alright because we've mistaken romance for compatibility and that's the 1990s' fault, stop being so superficial. You get up to go to the bathroom, and I start thinking about my tax return and the pair of jeans I've left in my checkout cart online. My phone goes. It's a message from you. I wonder if it's delayed from before we met and entered the restaurant. I have nothing else to do with my eyes or hands so I open it. It's not. It reads 'ur cool'. I put my phone face down on the table and pretend I haven't seen it.

You're back and talking about someone you used to date who lived in 'B', which I assume stands for Berlin, Germany, but I don't ask. You go into more depth about her love for fragrance design and how it completely changed your perspective on the world, look, here's a photo of the counter of cologne you now keep at home. While you're talking and showing me pictures on your phone, I'm thinking about why you decided to wear this very specific pair of shoes tonight. They're slip-ons, but not any slip-ons – they're like what my dad wore to mow the lawn in 1997. I'm wondering about the precise moment you walked out the door and thought, 'I'll just slip these on.' I can hear them slipping on under the table. I need to shut up and open my mind if I ever want to fall in love. I smile and say, wow, she seems cool.

Dinner's come and gone and I tried not to eat too much, too fast, or let the colours of the meal stain around my mouth, which is surprisingly easy as you haven't asked me a question in about 17 minutes. Maybe it's less. It could be less. It could be more like five, but it feels like a long time. I experiment with bringing up the subject of my job, which I quite like and would enjoy talking about in the same way I talk about everyone else's ideas all day, but it seems to bore you, so we return to the intricate details of other areas in your life you've optimised. I nod and say that's so interesting, tell me more. I wonder how I can find out whether or not you sleep on a mattress on the floor without having to explicitly ask you what your bedroom looks like.

It's 8:57pm and I'm thinking about ordering another glass of wine because I've finished mine, but you haven't finished yours. Is it tacky if I have another, or is that what a confident woman would do? I want to message my friends and ask, but that's rude, and I don't want you to know I've read the text you sent from the bathroom. Plus, I have to be totally in the moment here. I take another sip and we move onto the subject of a life-changing trip you once took to Brooklyn, New York. I decide on the additional wine and, while you're talking, I'm thinking about how much work I have to do tomorrow and whether I should pick up a bottle of sparkling water and a block of Dairy Milk on the way home to offset my potential hangover and feeling of disillusionment. Dating is going to give me diabetes.

Now they're clearing our plates, and I'm thinking about what other people are thinking when they see us at this fusion restaurant that promises midweek anonymity and inoffensive meals for less than $25, which I know I shouldn't be thinking about. I should be thinking about you in some future potential state and whether I'd want to, say, leave you in the kitchen at a party, or trust you with my bank card in your inside jacket pocket, or post a slightly obscured photo of you in three months' time with a caption that just says something like 'Saturday'. Instead, I'm wondering how the couple next to us got together and whether she wishes she was me right now, seemingly on the precipice of some wild sex with a stranger in unfortunate shoes. Little does she know I'll be in bed with a makeup wipe in 27 minutes if I can time this right.

Dinner's over, and we're outside doing that awkward thing where we can't tell each other what either of us wants to do next. I'm wondering if I should deploy the elephant-in-the-room[12] approach and

---

12 Elephant-in-the rooming: The practice of saying out loud what you know everyone is thinking, or what you're worried or self-conscious about, in order to avoid an anxious spiral about what other people might be thinking.

straight up ask you what you want. But before I can, you pick my chin up with your hand like you've seen it in a Hugh Grant film and kiss me unpassionately on the lips. A bit of teeth. Slight stabby sensation with your tongue. For the four seconds we're kissing, I'm feeling a bit dead inside and wondering whether this affection is better than the stress relief I get from leaving the office to buy a second coffee. I mean, I don't dislike you. But it doesn't feel the way I'm pretty sure it should. But, then again, a friend of mine met a boring guy for a drink once and persisted with hanging out, and now they co-own a dog and their lives look pretty good. We stop kissing, or maybe I stop kissing you, and say cutely, yeah, yeah, let's hang out again soon, hug, and walk away. It takes all my strength not to immediately pull out my phone and dramatically regale the story of the entire uneventful night to the group chat.

I'm home now and thinking about the kiss, which in hindsight actually has made me feel alive and like maybe it was all worth it. Although I'd quite happily never message you again and run into you at a fresh produce market in six months time, where you'll have your arms around a girlfriend who suits you better than me. Although, maybe that would make me jealous and I should give you another chance . . . I'm thinking about all of this and what to do next, but I'm tired and a bit tipsy, so I set my phone down next to my bed. A notification pings in the app from someone I haven't met in real life yet. 'U up?' I switch my phone to silent, put it face down on the table and pretend I haven't seen the message.

Romance is soft launching your crush on the internet

Romance is losing track of time.
Romance is risking anything when I could be home on the couch.
Romance is your hands in my unwashed hair and not caring.
Romance is the way you say my name.
Romance is the way I fantasise my future.
Romance is what's happening when no one's watching.
Romance is doing something otherworldly with my body.
Romance is slowly folding the fitted sheet, putting it in the drawer and hoping you'll be back again.
Romance is why I won't reply for a little while so we can keep the mystery.
Romance is what the light just did.
Romance is making the world softer.
Romance is not going slowly about it.
Romance is my own time.
Romance is you being obsessed with me.
Romance is in the tiny details.
Romance is you, who I love, and me, who I'm learning to.
Romance is breaking all my rules.
Romance is wanting to keep this a secret so I don't jinx it.
Romance is me changing your life.

Romance is what makes your eyes go soft.

Romance is your hand on the small of my back, not in an 'I own her' way but in a 'this feels nice' way.

Romance is lucky, can I have some?

Romance is taking a photo of you on my couch to prove that you exist.

Romance is your name on my lock screen.

Romance is how did you get that? I want it, too.

Romance is so much to celebrate if I could just clear this work off my desk.

Romance is doing something with my hands.

Romance is leaping into this feeling, because I'll never get this moment back.

Romance is gumption mixed with horny behaviour.

Romance is lighting my stupid little candles, making my stupid little vision board and genuinely believing some of it will come true.

Romance is going to save us if we let it.

Romance isn't wasting my time, it's how I'm filling my life.

Good Love is coming for you
By Bel

Gamification of romantic hell, present day

There's crushing, baiting, orbiting, benching, pedestalling, breadcrumbing, and every other mind-bending stage in nowomansland between being alone and being together, which is why you shouldn't take romantic advice from someone who hasn't been on a date since 2012 and therefore has never used a dating app. Because if they haven't, they'll want to take your phone and swipe through the lottery, pour a large glass of Sauvignon Blanc and indulge vicariously in your late-night alleyway make-outs with someone-fine-but-forgettable, talk about how they miss the thrill of the chase, and two hours later get picked up by their partner who's waiting in a hybrid SUV at the bottom of the driveway.

Despite the maze of people holding fish or posing in front of sedated tigers, group shots when you can't tell which person you're talking to, and people looking for a 'side partner not to tell their primary about,' we need to know that Good Love exists. It's just not what it used to be, because the apps act like a romantic slot machine, making us think that someone better, smarter and more beautiful is one more seductive tap away. I know Good Love exists because I've experienced it myself.

I know, I know. Good Love can be so boring to read about because it's like when someone comes back from holiday and wants to show you their photos, even though you've seen them posted for the last three weeks while you were getting up in the dark, making coffee with damp hair running down your back and rushing to get to work on time. It gives: 'If you're lucky enough, someone will want to do this with you one day too! Just keep swiping!' The apps were such a thrill when they first came out because we believed they were now the masters of our romantic destinies. And then they turned into a game we all had to learn to play.

A date once told me that his five-man flat would link up Tinder to their TV and sit in their lounge scrolling through each of their feeds. We expect dating app feeds to act like news feeds, constantly updated with something urgent or shiny and new we should know about. No wonder we're in a gumption epidemic – the here and now is no longer enough. As I left his house the following morning, I passed the room where four couches in various colours of depressed teal were laid out like a grandstand around the large television. The thought of being up on that screen ranked by a group of boys eating mi goreng in their track pants has never left me. I never returned.

One holiday season, almost every second person who swiped on my friends' profiles was dressed in some sort of Santa paraphernalia. Naked in a Santa apron. At a Christmas party in a slutty Santa outfit. Curled up as an elf under the tree. The evidence of this period was mostly ephemeral and lives on deep in the archives of a group chat we affectionately named 'Pick Your Fighter'. It ended when someone's former teacher swiped on them, and we realised we'd nearly clocked the local romantic internet like a level on a game, and there were no new contenders left. There's no wonder falling in love feels more complicated than ever, and older generations don't understand why we all want to go to therapy to work out our attachment style and what we've been doing wrong all this time. We can't easily forget about our exes because they're only ever just one tag popping up on our feeds away. We want love but we want it to be the right type and we want it to happen like it used to: serendipitously.

But in this mess of we-connected-instantly-and-messaged-nonstop-for-a-week-and-then-on-the-morning-of-our-first-date-they-never-responded escape rooms modern dating has created, we still have to believe in Good Love. We need stories that remind us there's this beating, living, heart-shaped thing in this body of ours that might just collide with another at any moment.

Mount Victoria, Wellington, New Zealand, 2020

When it happened, it was one of the greatest thrills of my life. Truly. You fall into Good Love and, all of a sudden, you get happier. Therapists can't tell you this because they can't guarantee it'll happen to you, but it's true. You just find yourself one evening, up late, hand-making pasta because you suddenly want to start cooking. You never liked cooking before. You start coming home from work to the music of someone in your kitchen, making dinner and pouring wine into two glasses. When Good Love came, it was, dare I say it – a giant relief. I had surfed in Morocco, got high in parks in Amsterdam, ridden on the backs of motorbikes through the flower markets of Hanoi and yet, this sweet, soft, mundane domesticity did something to me I never expected: it calmed me down. It made me feel like I fit.

My Good Love wore yellow t-shirts and wasn't preoccupied with new technology or elaborate lads' weekends; traits I found exotic and horny in 2020, given the onset of both soft boys and a bout of climate anxiety. He knew things like why cities were built in certain ways and how Napoleon made the French line their streets with trees so their soldiers could march in the shade over summer. Or how the tallest building in a given area represents, philosophically, the thing that area values most (where we lived, this was a casino, which we used to laugh about looking out at it from our rented balcony). Five years after we met, and nearly a year of long-distance slow falling in love later, I found a small 1970s apartment with sliding doors that opened onto the tree-tops for us to live in. It caught a kind of buttery evening light that convinced me being in love there would feel like a holiday and that all the loneliness I'd ever experienced in the world was over. And for a time, I was right. Good Love, in its beginning, is so gorgeous and naive like that. I hope that part never changes for anyone.

In the weeks before we moved in together, I grew so nervous I was so independent I'd be a bad live-in lover, that I started conducting informal interviews with friends who had long-term partners.

'What about Sundays? What do you do on Sundays?'

'Um – Sundays are the best because you get to be either those couples at brunch you've spent your entire single life resenting or hungover rats eating burgers in bed till 3pm with no one else around.'

'Do you think he'll find it cringe that I like cute things? Like this vase [holds up vase in video chat]?'

'No.'

'What if he thinks I'm basic for re-watching *Sex and the City* season three?'

'Dump him.'

'Do you still have sex? What do you do if they stop finding you hot?'

'Are you done yet?'

Excruciating to think we can find someone who makes us feel so at home yet still believe our humanness will be the thing that lets us down.

And then Good Love does its infallible thing: it defies all logic and changes your life. Being in Good Love was the luckiest I've ever felt because I finally got to be the girl in the movie and not the one scrolling past another photo dump 'with this one'. I was the one. The one with someone's arm around my back in public and wanting it to be there, being bought cheap flowers to put in that cute vase at the side of my bed, and waking up to the noise of two coffee cups clinking; the sound of someone loving me being awake.

During this time, I was working in an office at the top of a tall glass building that looked over a main road. I was bored in my job, but happy in my life (as often seems to be the way) and I spent a lot of my time staring out the window, watching the woman who owned the convenience store across the street. Every day at about one o'clock, once the sun started to creep into her doorway, she'd pull a milk crate out in front of her shop, turn it over and sit on it with her shoes off, eyes closed, face into the sun. Customers would have to take their time. The traffic could fuck off. The world could wait. I always thought that's what Good Love felt like. We cycled past her on our way home one afternoon, and I was sure I caught her eye outside her shop right before the lights changed. I swear in that fleeting encounter, her face read, 'Bel, don't blink – don't miss it.' I wanted to give Good Love everything I could.

Aside from the obvious perks, like someone to split dinners with and wear a simple lick of mascara on date night for, there were things about my friends who were in couples behaviour that started to make sense. Why they wouldn't text back in reliable rhythms on the weekends. Why they always had family events or dinners to attend. On top of that, the most boring, mundane things become fun. Things like sitting in the sun on the floor of your apartment on a Sunday afternoon, *just sitting*; legs entangled and the washing drying in the most beautifully domestic way possible. No one prepares you for this feeling. It's insane. Going to Kmart to buy a rubbish bin feels exciting. *Our* rubbish bin. That goes under *our* sink. Where *our* taps turn on. You start to hear yourself saying, 'I'll see what we're up to that weekend,' like it's always been that way – it literally just slips out of your mouth before you know you've done it. After a visit to my parents, my dad watched us pulling out the driveway, headed back home to carry on, as he put it, 'knitting our lives together'. We were the needle, Good Love was the wool.

But in Good Love, something else happens. You run out of time. You wake up on a lazy Saturday morning and your group chat with your friends is already 12 unread messages deep, and they're meeting somewhere to do something, and you don't want to escape your bubble. You can't keep up. You were once a Good Friend with time to video call from the changing room of a sample sale, sit up late and help proofread a job application or rush round with a bottle of supermarket Chardonnay as soon as disaster struck. But in the initial throws of Good Love, you can't do those things, because you're busy. Being in love. Good Friends will let you go and, if you're a Good Friend, when you stop feeling like the first person who's ever felt this way before, eventually you'll come back.

These are unavoidable trade-offs that we make in exchange for love. We can't be everything for everyone all at once, and the Good Love feeling is so alluring it makes it so hard not to abandon ourselves. I had spent so much time running my career and pouring myself into friendships that falling in love with someone sweet was like putting the car in neutral and gliding down the hill with the windows down. To have someone say, *slow down and be here, make a small life with me* felt like the most romantic directive I could ever receive. We have to enjoy these moments. But we also mustn't forget the person we were before them.

Wedding, New Zealand, 2022

If I hear, 'It'll happen to you when you least expect it' one more time, I'm going to fill my pockets with stones and walk into the sea. It's this and other stupendous lies that tie us in knots over what we're doing or not doing to attract love in our lives. Whether it's believing we're worth it, working hard enough to get it or looking glowed-up enough for someone to hit on and decide they'll take a chance, these lies make it feel like we're never going to experience Good Love.

You will know this if you've ever been single at a wedding, which is both an incredibly fun thing because you don't have to worry about your partner having a good time and a joyful form of altruistic community-service level of devotion to your friends getting married. Especially when you get cold and have no one's jacket to borrow and end up making small talk with a table of their random relatives.

'Wow and so you just live on your own?'

'Do you have a job?'

'Did you think of bringing a friend tonight?'

'Have you tried dating apps?'

'Have you met Nathan, the groomsman? He drives a Hilux and owns a few hectares in a verrry good part of town.'

And then you hear the cover band strike up 'Wagon Wheel', and you're allowed to politely pick up your tiny handbag, take a piece of cake and Irish Goodbye from the evening.

So how can we know that Good Love will happen to us? The truth is that we can't. The truth is that it might show up in your life as traditional romance, or it might take a different shape altogether. When we take Good Love down from the top of life's triangle of achievements, it becomes a thing but not *the* thing in our lives. It lives alongside all the other important life milestones and triumphs, and we can set ourselves free from the idea that we have to be chosen by someone else in order to fully exist.

Although, this is easier in theory than practice. One of the most common anxieties we have about life when we half-live through online windows into everyone else's happiness is a desperate wish to know when love will happen to us. But if we knew that, we'd also have to know answers to all the other existential realities, too, like when we'll die, where we'll eventually end up living and how much money we'll make. We're so used to knowing how many steps we've taken, might take, probably will take, how long before the car arrives and where exactly they're circling on the map to try and find us, how many times people have looked at our posts, and what people are saying about a certain dish at a restaurant, that we expect to carry this level of data into the feeling parts of our lives. It's so annoying and it's such an uncontrollable truth, but in order to keep some of the magic left in the world, some things need to be left unknown until they happen. Good Love is one of them.

Santo António, Lisbon, Portugal 2023

Two years after the end of Good Love and three failed attempts at turning the apps back on and off in sync with my waxing and waning will to (romantically) live, I meet Peggy at a tech event neither of us are really interested in. She's glamorous in that casually content way someone in love is. We immediately bond and instead of activating the QR code to access the portal that will predict our AI future, we spend the whole night talking about the new love she's just fallen into after . . . being accidentally cc-d on an email. 'Isn't that insane?!' she says, 'that things like that still happen? You think it's all over and then you get a notification in your inbox like a Meg Ryan film'. I check my empty lockscreen, just in case.

'It's incredible,' I say, draining my drink, 'The simple power of the cc – they write books about this shit!' And I mean it. And I'm jealous. And in awe. And embarrassed that I've become hardened by the commodification of modern love the way Esther Perel warns us about in that 47-second clip from a podcast episode. The thought of having my heart broken again makes me want to swallow a scented candle.

'I know,' she says. She's glistening in that sweet way I remember from my own halcyon Good Love days and I want that feeling back. I love that she believes in it. 'I'm 57! I feel 15! How insane is that! There I was, just building my own life, and then, bang! Anything – and I mean anything – really does happen,' she says and her Apple Watch lights up with a new message from him. I tell her the most romantic thing that's been done for me is being sent a photo by a French man of a fruit platter with the strawberries arranged to spell my name. She says that's cute, and I say, 'I think if I get my heart broken again I might die. But in the same breath, it's extremely depressing if that's the last romance I'll ever get.'

'Oh, babes – you never want to regret trying anything! Besides, you could fall into Good Love and something else in life will break your heart. We can never predict anything!' God it's so annoying when happy strangers are right.

We were both drinking the free mocktails all night, which is how I can be sure everything she said was true. The truth was written all over her: Good Love is a relief. It feels like peace. It's what happens before the photographs, and the parties and the moments we think we deserve. In all the weddings I've spoken at, written vows for, officiated and attended, wondering if or when it'll ever happen to me in that Big Way, I've come to know this: Good Love does not require perfection in order for you to find it – it makes its way through your humanness. I've never sat at a trestle table opposite two people in love, who've said, 'I was just feeling really complete, and then we met'.

We have to give a little more credit to the chaos of life. I made the mistake in my twenties of sectioning my life into perfectionist marketing phases in the lead up to the main event when Good Love was supposed to arrive. This is both my fault and that of every adult who looks at people flying solo like they've lost in the modern gamification of love. It's like: *I'm fine, but once my hair grows, once I have enough savings, once I have a perfect body, once I pay off my debts, once that family thing works itself out, once I have an outfit that makes me look both flawless and approachable – then the time will come.* This perfect time never arrives. When that falling moment comes, though – don't question it. Take a bite of that bespoke fruit platter and let juice drip down your chin. Believe that love comes to you in its own distinct shape that might not be what you were looking for or led to expect. And when it crashes in, turn your face to the sun. Hold onto it like light.

TEXT OR CALL?

FADE IN:

EXT. STREET - NIGHT

A small crowd of animated eople spill out onto the busy street of an inner-city music venue. A reggae cover band plays inside. It's hot. Everyone's boisterous and happy. Two people kiss on the footpath in the middle of it all, unphased by the festivities around them.

An expensive car drives past and toots its horn.

                        CRUSH 1
               (stops kissing, but still close)
        That could be your boss driving past.

                        CRUSH 2
    I don't care.

A DRUNK GUY yells 'WO-WOO!' from across the street.

                    CRUSH 2 (CONT'D)
          That could be your ex.
                         CRUSH 1
              (smiling and taking a step back, taking it
                            all in)
          I don't care.

A beat. The band inside strikes up a cover of
'Shake It Off'. It's not good. Neither of them
notice. Neither want to move.

                       CRUSH 1 (CONT'D)
          So you're, um, quite cool.

                         CRUSH 2
              (also smiling and also stepping back)
          Am I just?

                         CRUSH 1
          Yes. It's, um. Quite rare.

CRUSH 1 runs his fingers through his hair and bites
his lip awkwardly.

                         CRUSH 2
          Question. Do you use 3-in-1?

                         CRUSH 1
              (surprised, but laughing)
          What? No.

CRUSH 2

What about a mattress on the floor?

CRUSH 1

Again, no.

CRUSH 2

Polyamorous?

CRUSH 1

No!

CRUSH 2

Hmmm. You're right. This is rare. And I feel very alive but also very drunk and it's 2am so I think I'm going to go home. (beat) Alone.

CRUSH 1 pulls out his phone and orders a ride. CRUSH 2 looks flustered. Within seconds, it pulls up.

CRUSH 1

That's me.

CRUSH 2

Wait! Can I have your number?
I have a feeling this shouldn't end here.

CRUSH 1 takes his phone and punches her number in, saving it under a wine glass emoji so he'll have to go looking for it before handing the phone back and opening the car door and sliding inside.

                    CRUSH 2 (CONT'D)
          One last thing before you go —

The driver beeps her horn. CRUSH 1 hovers between the car door and its interior.

                         CRUSH 1
          Of course.

                    CRUSH 2 (CONT'D)
          Text — or call?

                         CRUSH 1
                         (smiling)
          Call. Definitely always call.

CRUSH 1 closes the car door and the car pulls away.

END.

Horny behaviour

Organises something, anything (preferably fun and not oriented around their own hobby). Calls you. On your phone number. Like it's a normal thing to do. Owns a car or mode of transport that requires servicing, and possesses the ability to operate it. Remembers your friends' names. Enters the party with you, leaves with you, genuinely content in between. Can hold a conversation with a parent without you worrying. Likes to dance or watches you dance without getting jealous. Gets jealous, but in a cute way. Naturally possesses gumption. Can navigate an airport or emergency situation with relative ease. Goes to the bathroom at a restaurant and comes back after secretly paying. Knows how to stalk your internet behaviour well enough to know what to buy you for your birthday. Your friends don't lie about not minding when they come too. Dotes on you when you're sick. Buys you cheap flowers often, rather than expensive bouquets once a year. Carries something of yours (the burden may be emotional or physical) without complaining. Exhibits the characteristics of being able to build a retaining wall or offer it emotionally. Can choose and book somewhere for dinner without turning the decision into a 30 message exchange. Extravagant in small ways. Really loves a hobby that isn't protein-related or riding the NASDAQ. Brings you coffee in bed. Doesn't use not having checked their phone as an excuse for not texting back. Believes in things against all odds. Treats you like a finite resource.

Unhorny behaviour

Ownership of thin-soled Chuck Taylors with low-cut socks peeking out the top. Tells their mother their secrets instead of you. Forgets important dates regularly. Says, 'Yeah the boys!' unironically. Intentionally can't figure out their Google calendar so they don't have to organise things. Doesn't tell their friends they love them. Is over 20 and still listens to trap music. Feathery touching while you're hungover or half-asleep. Is obsessed with either New York or Berlin or both. Can't think about the future but claims they always want to go 'on adventures'. Owns heaps of cologne but doesn't buy you anything, like not even a chocolate bar at the 7/11. Can't make you something to drink unless it's from a can. Uses the phrase 'this one' as social media captions. Sleeps in dark-coloured sheets that likely pre-date their first job. Uses a twisted string of plastic wrap as a belt. Gets dating app notifications while you're out for dinner. DMs you incessantly but never calls. Is never busy. Thinks you can't understand their work. Doesn't say thank you. Ignores you around their friends. Talks over you. Doesn't vote. Showers too often. Showers . . . never. Thinks your star sign is unfortunate. Would not be a good partner in *The Amazing Race*.

CHAPTER 7

Staying sane in the matrix

Surviving online, living in the real world and keeping OK in here.

Tapping in, tapping out
By Lucy and Bel

'OK. What are our first memories of using the internet?' We ask each other before we start to write this chapter.

Setting up my own Bebo account with *Skins*-themed wallpaper and changing the rankings of my top 16 friends with ruthless social analysis.

Getting the email addresses of boys during a school trip only to indulge in months of back-and-forth instant messaging, never to meet each other in real life again.

Setting up my dolphins2themax Hotmail address with no sense that it would be permanent.

Sitting on the family computer in my dad's office waiting to use the dial-up internet while he was on the phone to some man about the price of sheep.

Having entire classes at school learning how to 'effectively' ask Google a question.

A random guy telling me he'd end it all if I stopped replying to him on *Habbo Hotel*.

A random guy who wanted me to send him a photo of myself and to know if I liked Panic! At The Disco.

A random guy pretending he was Nick Jonas and 'proving' it by walking me through his diabetes diagnosis.

People follow you online because they want something out of you, not to give something back. It's become so pervasive, this expectation to be constantly making, that we have to make sure there's something left of ourselves beyond ephemeral online moments.

The internet entered our lives early enough that we're considered 'digital natives', but late enough that we knew a world where 'going online' was an activity and not a state of being. Knowing that we may be the last generation to have this offline-online existence is a privilege we don't take lightly, which is why we're here.

What once felt like a book where you'd seamlessly glide from page to page – from a Wikipedia page listing sexually active popes one minute to someone's personal emo Tumblr the next – has turned into something else entirely. A whole other world. It's a diary. It's a vengeance. It's where the worst human thoughts go to circulate and feel important. It's where you discover the best ideas and people if you look hard enough. You make one mistake out there, and you (and your whole livelihood) can be cancelled in an instant. You do one thing right and you could be set up for life. But as much as we've harnessed this seemingly all-knowing monster, we're still left with some questions that not even a perfectly structured Google search can give us the answer to.

Has all this connection made us any more connected?

If the younger versions of ourselves who would literally say 'brb' to our friends each time we jumped offline to go and use the bathroom could see us now, they'd be alarmed at the unread messages we've got stacking up, even though we're on our phones, like all the time.

Would I have been better off without the internet?

Sure, it was jarring to become a sentient teenager and realise we were social media's guinea pigs, feeling our way through the shadowy parts and hoping we escape unscathed. In the same breath, we wouldn't be here without turning everything we learnt as internet crash test dummies into something beautiful.

Am I ugly/boring/mediocre or am I just staring at other people's lives too much?

The latter.

Some of us are totally screened out, some of us have found communities of people who've saved our lives and, well, some of us owe our whole careers to this thing.[13] The internet is a beautiful fractured mirror where most of us live at least some aspect of our short time on this planet. The key is figuring out how we can be on the internet and still like what's reflected back at us. brb x

---

13 Screening out: the full zombie catatonic mode you enter when you've been staring at a small, medium or large screen (sometimes all three) for too long.

The Shrinking Years
By Lucy

'I hate my body. I hate myself. I'm not eating and I don't even care. On the bright side, I hit 17.9k followers on Twitter!' It's the 9th of June in 2013, and I'm 15 years old.

The first memory I have of my weight being a problem is in the sunroom of my childhood home. Mum sat me down and gently told me I was going to the doctor to get some tests done to see whether I had 'something called diabetes'. I couldn't have been any older than five, so I was bribed with the promise of a surprise afterwards. In the end we both got one: I received a *Sabrina the Teenage Witch* magazine, and Mum received test results telling her that I didn't have diabetes, she just had a chunky kid.

Since then, not a day has gone by where I haven't thought about how I look. I spent my formative years trialling every 'challenge' or 'programme' I could find in my small town. I made my dad take me to fitness boot camps before school and my mum cook me completely separate meals from my brothers. I traded in my subscription to *Dolly* magazine for the *Healthy Food Guide*, which told me to cut out a new food group with each month's issue, and I visited naturopaths who told me that, along with sugar and gluten, I should stay away from dairy products too.

I hated shopping and how I'd have to dig to the bottom of every pile of jeans to find a pair that might fit or ask an assistant to help me grab the coathanger at the very back. I cried in changing rooms, cried at the beach, cried in my bedroom every time I thought about Mum saying, 'A moment on the lips, a lifetime on the hips.' I was embarrassed when the kids at school yelled 'WHALE' at me as I walked across the school field to get home one day, and when I found the 'Wide Load Follows' sign in my brother's driving exam book had been crossed out and replaced with my name. I thought about how many almonds I was allowed to eat at once, how flat my stomach was in the morning versus the afternoon, how I was going to look in my netball dress compared to the other girls, and how to avoid people all summer. Being smaller was all I wanted, and my determination was completely wasted on it.

Let me tell you how this happens

It happens when you grow up watching an objectively beautiful Bridget Jones being referred to as 'overweight' for an entire movie franchise. It happens when you read magazine spreads solely dedicated to annotating celebrity cellulite, which births a fear that one day those circles and arrows might be pointed at you. It happens when the minutes between *The Biggest Loser* and *Project Runway* are stuffed with ads for Special K and Subway and WeightWatchers and Jenny Craig weight-loss plans and the new Ab King Pro. It happens when you get your first iPhone and start examining yourself from every angle.

In a way, I was lucky. My shrinking years started long before we all carried around a portal that let us see how we could be 'better' with every scroll, before the word 'selfie' had become so entrenched in the zeitgeist that Kim Kardashian had released a book of them. It was before we had lifestyle influencers or comment sections or the ability to zoom through our screens and into someone else's pores to feel better about our own. When the trolls are in real life, you can spot them. When they can shapeshift into whoever is trying to sell you skinny tea or not disclosing the latest surgery they've had or which miracle drug they've used to make them look a certain way, they're harder to escape.

Your social media diet

Self-optimised people use the term 'social media diet' to talk about the periods when they delete their apps and take a break from the online world. They write articles about 'cutting out' certain sites or 'restricting their consumption' to form a 'healthy' relationship with the web. They stand on stage and preach about what all this 'toxic' and 'sugary' content will do to us if we don't start 'exercising restraint'. The language here is not lost on me. 'Social media dieting' is something people choose to do when they're older and can afford to make mindfulness their hobby. For young people online, a different kind of social media diet chooses you.

I was 15 the first time I used a front-facing camera or visited an app store. There my iPhone linked me to my two new confidants and mentors: Tumblr and Twitter. I joined these platforms to show my adoration for One Direction, and they showed me something quite different in return. On Tumblr, I logged on in search of friends or fanfiction and was instead introduced to the concepts of 'grunge' and 'thinspiration.' The two concepts were in cahoots because grunge was as much a fashion trend as it was a body type – one that required girls like me to make 'thinspo' our new religion. There were depths to our dashboards, and down there it was beautiful, beautiful suffering. It was all ripped tights, thigh gaps and stylised quotes from Kate Moss telling me that 'nothing tastes as good as skinny feels'.

Every reblog suppressed my appetite a little bit more, stuffing my brain with useless information that I'll never be able to shake, like how to eat as little as possible at Thanksgiving (a holiday we don't even celebrate in New Zealand) or how much exercise I'd need to do to work off the calories in soy milk. I became dependent on Tumblr to 'keep me on track', and for analogue moments, like when I had no wifi or my iPod had been confiscated, I'd even printed some of my favourite posts and glued them into an old exercise book labelled 'science' that I hid under my bed.

If Tumblr was for starving, Twitter was for filling back up. It introduced me to the sugar substitute I was so desperately seeking, in the sweet, sweet rush of likes and retweets. It taught me about dopamine and online validation, and that if I didn't have the prerequisites to be popular in real life, I could be popular there. I was hungry all the time. Hungry for more engagement. Hungry for the reply of a stranger. Hungry for more followers. It's like Twitter distracted me from thinking about my body, while Tumblr reminded me, with every scroll, that my body was all I should be thinking about. It was a doom cycle I didn't know I was trapped in. My follower counts went up, my calorie count went down.

Online, I was growing; on earth, I was disappearing. I didn't care. All those little doubts and insecurities I had about my nature or appearance in real life were being both validated and encouraged online. Of course I wasn't as smart as everyone else! Of course I should stop eating! Of course no one would notice if I disappeared!

I cosplayed that beautiful and sad girl online until she seeped into my real life and I no longer wanted to eat, or talk to my brothers, or, play my guitar, or see my friends. When this happened it felt like a success. Like it's what the internet wanted.

My friends asked why I didn't eat lunch anymore, and my mum took me to cafés to watch me force down a toasted sandwich, mouthful by mouthful. Whenever anyone suggested I took a break from the internet, I would snap that they didn't understand. Why would I give up the one place I was thriving? It's a shameful truth to admit that it wasn't the interventions from my friends or family that encouraged me to re-enter the real world and start valuing my offline life again, it was simply that I left the One Direction fandom and didn't return properly to the internet until I was in my twenties. By the time I came back, we'd graduated from those eras of Tumblr and Twitter and people were suddenly talking about being present and confident in our skin and touching grass. It didn't exactly seem better – just different.

The internet: mother, God or both?

As teenagers on the internet, we used to log on and think it was only our bodies that needed fixing. We lived through iteration after iteration of it: Thinspiration, Body Positivity, Body Acceptance, Body Neutrality, Fitspiration, Green Smoothies and Apple Cider Vinegar, Brazilian Butt Lifts, Brazilian Butt Lift reversals, FaceTune, Filters, Ozempic. The feed scrolls on.

Now we're told everything needs fixing. We open up our phones and a face fills the screen to tell us that a calorie deficit is the only way we'll be able to 'lose that stubborn extra belly fat'. That since we lose focus and zone out of conversations we have ADHD. That spearmint tea is the miracle treatment for our hormonal acne. That we're bisexual. That we should buy a ring light or the latest trending serum or get our lips done. That we need to be good enough, not for the people around us in our real lives, but good enough for the internet. Like the internet is our mother or God or our latest crush.

Algorithms have become our doctors, therapists, dieticians and stylists. It's like you wake up content with how your brain works and by the time you go to bed all you can think about is whether you'd be better on Ritalin because that one influencer told you it changed her life. It's a natural reaction to the unnatural situation we're in where healthcare is expensive, underfunded and under-staffed, certain areas are under-researched and some people get better treatment than others. For some of us, being able to find answers online can be life-changing. But for most of us, opening up an app on a random Tuesday for a nighttime reprieve from the world and being incidentally exposed to the idea that you might have three different undiagnosed conditions, isn't good for the psyche.

I'm on the internet more than I ever have been before, but the antidote has been building a platform that is completely divorced from looking cool online or being skinny in real life. De-centring yourself from your internet experience makes your time there meaningful. Get obsessed with the news. With a niche Scandinavian TV show. With blogging. With anything that doesn't require you to scrutinise your appearance or ask a stranger to move out of your shot. Understand that you're living with a full-length mirror in your pocket at all times, but the power lies in refusing to let it ruin your day or offer you 'solutions.' Understand that you have the power in the first place.

As I'm writing this in the library, I look up from my computer and see a girl around eight years old, who reminds me of myself. She's standing in the fiction section, probably about to take home more books than she's able to read. Her cheeks are pink, and she's wearing skinny jeans tucked into a pair of brown suede boots that look a few sizes too big for her. She's paired this look with a hoodie, and I can tell she's trying to seem grown up but is limited by her parents' schedule and the department stores in town. Something about her gives me hope that in a world full of 'get-ready-with me' videos and blushes and skin tints and serums and no-make-up-makeup, these kids still exist. I hope no one buys her an iPhone for as long as possible. I hope she gets to become herself in private before it's too late.

The internet's taken all my mystery and I want it back

LUCY: ok so what you just sent me for this weeks newsy about losing our mystery has sent me into a SPIRAL

                                                  BEL: Love having this effect
                                                                       But also
                                                                          Elaborate

LUCY: idk it just made me think about how the internet has ruined the 'get to know each other' phase
because we all just OVERSHARE
it's like there's nothing left
like the other night i was at a party and a guy didn't want to talk to me
because he 'didn't want to offend me' because of my 'woke' instagram
but then another guy pulled me into the bathroom to talk about gun reform
and i was like . . . ok neither of you should know any of this

                        BEL: Or like how when someone doesn't reply
                              I think it's because I've done something wrong

because I know we're all on our phones all the time
and I KNOW they're out doing things because I can
see them
Like a hawk
on the stupid internet
An internet hawk

LUCY: or like how I would never talk about my job on
a first date
because I don't want them googling me

BEL: Or finding something I've written!
About myself
About THE DATE
About ANYTHING
And then they think they know you
I should just start lying and say I work in tech
Because no one knows what that really entails

LUCY: no literally

BEL: I want to live under the thin veil of mystery for the rest of
my life
And yet
Here we are

LUCY: here we are
anyway
off to write about my deepest regrets in the newsy x

Doomscrolling

Don't spend your whole life being sucked into this thing, but if you can work hard enough, you can make it work for you. Don't be cringe, be funny and informative – it's not hard so get it right. Don't post on the wrong side of history, you'll never be forgiven. Find a healthy balance but don't you dare get so busy with your real life that you miss something important. Do you care or are you just virtue signalling? Prove it. Panic is making people crazy. 5G is making people crazy. And now if they're panicked and crazy they can share their opinions, too. Block. Unblock. Mute. Unmute. If you keep going like this, you'll get carpal tunnel syndrome from typing your life away and you'll never be able to hold a real-life pen again. It's 2024, will we even need pens again anyway? Be careful of the trolls, don't feed them because they'll bite back and then you'll end up on the 6 o'clock news. Don't make any mistakes or the internet is coming for you, we're all three online mistakes away from combustion. Your silence is complicit so figure out an in between that's both right and doesn't hurt anybody: good luck. Touch your screen and then go touch grass. Get some blue light from the sky and remember what is real. This is real, us, who you come home to. Text your friends back. Text your mum back. Text yourself a reminder to remember. Your next newsletter is scheduled for 5am; have a nice sleep.

Notifications

Olivia Rodrigo just followed you
Mark Zuckerberg replied to your Thread
Person you regrettably kissed one time liked your story
New comment: this is NOT shit I should care about
Reese Witherspoon just followed you
Email: Podcast request: Good Influence with Gemma Styles
New post: your old university friend soft launched their new crush by posting their hand across the table holding a beer
New comment: what do you know? Aren't you from New Zealand?
Ariana Grande just followed you
New comment from your distant family member asking after the family
Dua Lipa just followed you
New comment: why aren't you talking about [insert crisis here]
Chrissy Teigen mentioned you in her caption
Interview request: The cast of Mean Girls the Musical
Blake Lively just followed you
Joe Rogan just followed you *New comment: you took the words right out of my mouth, thank you xx*
DM from Brittany Broski
*New post: someone you don't really know anymore but haven't

gotten around to unfollowing is posing with a SOLD sign on their new home*
*Email: Join a virtual press conference with Jennifer Lopez'
DM from FINNEAS
New comment: damn, this page really fell off. unfollowing now.
Madonna just followed you

What you learn when you suddenly have three million followers
By Lucy

Good attention is like a drug

When you start to go 'viral' you can't sleep. You're up all night replying to every DM, comment, email. It's an inexplicable rush that you'll never be able to replicate. Once you get used to it, it will give you VERY unrealistic standards for each new post to live up to (only 10,000 likes? Flop). This amount of attention is not normal.

200k followers is the sweet spot

It will not always be good attention that you're getting. I've found that any more than 200k followers and people start to see you as a corporation instead of a person. They can say whatever they want to you because you're either Mark Zuckerberg or in a team of 50. You begin to lose the will to post.

You'll feel like Hannah Montana

If you do it right, you get the best of both worlds, where your real life feels very separate from your online one. Now and again though, they merge, and it will buzz you out. Like the time I met a girl on a small walking tour in a foreign country who excitedly told me she read my newsletter. Or when I got chatting to the lady next to me on a long-haul flight who just had to send all her friends a selfie when she found out who I was. My favourite was probably the dad who screamed in my face that he and his daughter love me at a tiny beach in New Zealand after he asked me what I did for work. Who would've thought that a girl like me would double as a superstar?

The internet incentivises people to take things in the worst way possible

There's a joke online that the quickest way to get an answer to any question is by posting something totally incorrect and letting the comments of people who 'know better' roll in. The only thing people love more than being right is when you're wrong, and they get the chance to tell you so. A term I love, 'the what about me effect', aptly describes how the algorithmic hell we live in has convinced us that everything we see should be perfectly tailored to us, which helps explain why people get so upset when something that doesn't directly pertain to them finds a way onto their feeds (and thus they must comment on it, obviously). It's helpful to remind yourself not to write with your worst critic in mind, or for an algorithm you might accidentally end up on.

The comments section never helped anything

Comments are great for validation and terrible for solving a historic and complex global crisis. Too much time in the comments section and you'll get hives. Hot tip: imagine someone in your real life sitting and commenting nasty things under people's photos and, when you realise you can't, log off and get in touch with a real life person. It also helps to remember that platforms want interaction and algorithms are built to encourage it. The trolls are in some way just doing what they've been subconsciously told to do.

Unless you're willing to sell yourself, you won't be rich

It's easy to see a big follower count and assume it equates to a stacked bank account. For some people, I'm sure that's the case, but when you don't show your face and aren't willing to pose with random products, your online activities will be a lot less profitable. And when you do find an organisation that aligns with your interests, some people will still be angry that you're 'capitalising on' the service you provide them for free every day. On the flip side, when you can't provide that service because you're working your café job, making money to keep your content free, people will be upset that you haven't covered everything that happened that day . . .

. . . and so you're damned if you do, damned if you don't

Best to get comfy with this ASAP. An idea that helped me come to terms with the fact that I'll never please everyone is 'stated preferences vs revealed preferences'. For example, some people will be VERY vocal when you post about things that they don't consider 'news,' yet every time you post a photo of Harry Styles it will perform at least five times better than any of your news-related posts. Don't let this dictate how you operate, but keep it in the back of your mind.

You'll be two degrees of separation from people you've obsessed over your entire life

Insane that being a fangirl online could lead to being trusted to host listening parties for Harry Styles or interview Lorde. Also insane to imagine that someone like Shania Twain is sitting in what I assume is a mansion somewhere, doing the same thing as all of us: sitting, scrolling and then hitting follow on some Kiwi chick's Instagram account on a random Friday morning. Or her assistant did, at least.

In the same way that you don't understand your best friend's office job, people won't really understand yours

A lot of people think they could do my job if they wanted to. They might suspect that my day consists of lounging around taking photos or getting dressed up for lunch with a skincare brand. That has never been my job. My job is great, but it also consists of news-induced screentime overload, pressure to always get everything right, trolls grumbling even when I do, inevitable hits to my self-confidence when I use the wrong word in a newsletter and hours of staying up trying to make sense of something complicated because someone in my DMs asked me to. I find it helpful to remind myself that if all those people really could handle doing this job, they'd be doing it.

People in your real life get realer

Your offline friends won't send you screenshots of what people are saying about you online. They'll remind you that no one you respect or trust in real life would say this to your face (or even think it) and that no matter how bad it gets, you're safe.

No one wins when you 'post through it'

At university we were taught that speed is everything in journalism, and that 'if it bleeds, it leads'. Turns out, that's not a good formula when it comes to social media. You'll really learn this when you watch a bunch of huge influencers (including the Prime Minister of Canada) share someone's 'viral' infographic that you personally fact-checked and found to be untrue. As hard as it is to ignore all the people in your DMs telling you that your silence is violence, it's ALWAYS better to make sure you're using your platform responsibly.

Low-stakes errors are actually the best things ever

Making small mistakes in public is humbling, but every time I do it, I'm glad. Not only does it remind people that you're human, but being in a constant feedback loop means you really learn to put your pride aside and admit when you've got something wrong. Also, making a low-stakes error is pretty good for engagement, because EVERYONE will let you know.

THE BEST PART OF ALL OF THIS IS YOU

You send messages of encouragement, leave a comment that something 'changed your life' and tell me you don't give a shit if I take a break. You don't care about engagement rates or typos or the 'consistency of posts'. You vote in our polls and submit your stories and send me updates about what's happening in your country. You don't know what I look like, but you don't care about that. You try to bring grace to the internet. You help me stay sane in the matrix.

Validation: the internet giveth, the internet taketh away

Olivia Rodrigo unfollowed you
Reese Witherspoon unfollowed you
Dua Lipa unfollowed you
Ariana Grande unfollowed you

And here I was, thinking I'm the only one
By Bel

You make me want to go to the party and not sit at home in the dark

'I need to pee.'
'Just pee on the street.'
'That's such a Rat Girl thing to do.'
'Who cares – I'll distract anyone who looks.'
I pee on the street.
No one looks.
We laugh and run on.

Alice and I meet as strangers who'd DM'd each other after stumbling across each others' Instagram profiles, noticing we lived in the same city and wondering if we would be friends. We meet, and it's the holy grail of female friendship: you hate all the same things, time passes without you noticing, and the next morning you wake up with a half-eaten bag of fries scattered next to your bed and a sentimental message on your phone screen you'd typed but hadn't sent. We arrange to go to a record store party a few weeks later, because this is the joy of the internet: you can expedite the process of getting to know someone before you've even met them.

The night of the party, we're on the street outside, checking we have the right address. Riding the high of making a new friend, I say, 'Hey, thanks so much for inviting me out. Am I cool? Do you think this is cool? Can we be friends?'

She laughs and threads her arm into mine, and we walk inside: she has handed me the keys to a whole new city.

So much is said about the perils of being online; that each post is doing volunteer work for the men who own the platforms, that you're handing over your mystery by trying to look good enough to be there in exchange for public displays of affection. But we can also look at it a different way: when we're ourselves online, it can become place of self-expression, experimentation and a way to attract people into our real lives who see themselves similarly. It's similar to how we align ourselves with film characters, except the internet opens up the ability to connect in real life. Put like that, being ourselves online can have a positively magnetic effect.

Just thought you should know, in case you had an existential crisis and thought about giving up

My Spotify Wrapped arrives, and I'm tipsy on a long-haul flight across the hemispheres. The animated email makes me feel special, like I've received personalised mail and achieved something huge; I'm in the top 3 per cent of listeners of a few musicians, making me a super fan. I've never been a super fan of anything. I've never queued for hours or made posters to wave at a show. I've never entered a chat room of people dissecting lyrics to songs as though they're clues to the secrets of the world. I wonder if this is because I grew up in a town where boys played rugby and everyone watched and it was embarassing to be obsessed with anything else. I'm feeling sentimental.

High on the power of my new status, I open my Notes app and draft a DM to a lesser-known musician on the list. I'm thinking, 'Imagine if they didn't know this?' I'm nowhere and no one, on a flight, moving between two continents in my anonymous life. They're on stage somewhere, waking up with a whisky hangover or in a café writing in a tiny notebook. As I recover from my jetlag in the days to come, I will cringe and regret this, but that's the future and this is now.

Dear [famous musician]

Firstly, I hope you get so many of these you don't even see this in your inbox.

Secondly, I wonder if it ever gets tiring, reading fan mail or feeling like people are obsessed with you. Maybe that's a nice feeling.

Anyway, I just wanted to say I love your music and please keep making it. I walked across a whole country once and listened to your albums the whole way. Amazing when you think about it – your music travelling so far and having such an effect on someone's life. Just thought you should know, in case you had an existential crisis and thought about giving up.

Supermarket apps and tech start-ups love to talk about their 'unique authentic communities' as though they're curing the loneliness epidemic. But nothing can beat the quiet, ridiculous gumption the internet gives a girl to think, just for a moment, they're one connection away from changing someone's life

Me after getting a sentimental DM from a stranger: I love being alive and maybe love exists and that this is all worth it

I can't sleep. It's early and hot. I open my phone and see my inbox has 17 unread emails, which is weird for 5:17am. Out of habit, I check our Substack, and Lucy and I have accidentally published a deeply personal essay I'd drafted for the Newsy but was too scared to send to 80,000 people. I feel like I'm going to throw up. I feel like I've just uploaded an album of 37 nudes on Facebook. I open the first email.

> guys – i'm writing this so fast my hands can't keep up i just want to tell you as soon as i read your story that you've put words to such big feelings of mine i never knew i had. my cheeks were wet with tears, it was like. . . she gets it. she gets it! please don't stop doing this! thank you xx

There are days where I feel like a gnawed-at skeleton from writing deeply personal things online. The feeling makes me want to delete everything. It makes me want to open a turtle sanctuary on a remote island and never be seen again. And then I have these cosmic-feeling moments, not because what I've written is particularly profound or will ever be quoted on Goodreads or in an English Literature degree essay, but because something I wrote went out into the world in that instantaneous way, and it reached someone, at that precise time, who needed it most.

File>Move to>Folder> Cute messages for bad days

Reaching online/real-life nirvana

When I was very young, and by that I mean before I was 13 and had my first cell phone, I thought 'community' was something very provincial. Like zip-off capri pants or fundraisers in the school hall, it implied spending weekends doing things your parents wanted you to do while you wished you were with your friends doing more important things, like curating your personal style.

At its coolest, 'community' was the five fans of my high-school band coming to watch us play at a smoke-free fundraiser for a Christian holiday programme. Even then, I didn't care about the cause; I was busy being a girl in a rock band worshipping Meg from The White Stripes. In my naivety, I believed there was something embarrassing about needing other people. I preferred the idea that true individuality – a concept I was obsessed with for a long time, the way teenagers so often are – only needed its own energy to survive.

But the more online I've become, the more I've come to know the opposite. Like many other soft, good things, the word 'community' has been co-opted by brands for long enough that it's no wonder our minds inextricably drift to some chocolate lovers' Facebook group or a suburb's group chat when we hear it. But there's something that happens at the intersection of our online and real selves that's undeniable: it makes what used to be impossible, possible.

To have a community is to know there's a light on (either physically or digitally); somewhere you can go and meet with others who make you feel less alone in the world. It's another space away from marinating in your own algorithmic angst,[14] that makes you stop thinking about yourself so much and feel connected to others by your shared love or need for something else. Communities are what we need to know others just like us exist.

---

14 Algorithmic angst: The uncomfortable feeling that you are being controlled by what the algorithms are serving you and the fear that they're shaping your understanding of the world.

Screening out
By Lucy

Sorry, but imagine explaining to a Victorian child that every night you sit in front of a large screen on the wall, with a medium-sized screen on your lap, a small screen in your hands and, because you're rich enough, a tiny screen on your wrist.

The large screen is playing a dating show where eight women aged between 40 and 60 are trying to find love. They're living in a villa in Mexico and, in this episode, they've just been told the people they're going to be dating are each other's sons.

On your medium screen, you're supposed to be answering the emails you didn't get to at work today, but they're lost somewhere in the jungle of tabs you've had open for a week. You can't possibly close them – there's an article about climate change in there somewhere that you know you should read. You feel your lap burning and hear a whirring sound that makes you think something is about to take flight. Your laptop needs a rest. So do you. You pick up the smaller screen.

Finally, something engaging! With less than ten strokes of your thumb, you've seen a photo of your cousin's wedding, someone from high school's engagement, a natural disaster displacing millions of people, some celebrity beefing with a child, an explainer on ways the world is burning, and your favourite musician holding a puppy. You only spent a few seconds hovering over each post (except, if you're honest, the wedding one, because you wanted to see the dress) even though, in the back of your mind, you knew that some of the content required more of your time and energy. You couldn't go back and read them if you tried. They've whooshed away into the mess of it all. You make a pact with yourself that you'll properly read the next infographic you see, even if it has typos. You might even share it to make yourself feel better than everyone else for a second. Actually, never mind, you've just noticed that some person you've never met hasn't posted a photo with their partner in a while, so you spend the rest of the evening scrolling back through their content to figure out if, when, why and how they broke up.

The tiny screen on your wrist buzzes, telling you it's time to 'stand up' and reminding you that you haven't gotten enough steps in today. You can't believe you actually pay for this kind of attention. You decide you'll slip the tiny screen into the pocket of your flatmate's shorts before they head to the gym so you can get a break from this surveillance AND get your step count up. This is working smarter, not harder. You should tweet about it.

You reach the end of all 16 of your feeds, which signals that it's time for bed and the onset of full goblin zombie catatonic mode, also known as 'Screening Out'. As per usual, the remnants of your pesto pasta will remain on the floor until the morning, and it takes every inch of your willpower to get up and brush your teeth. By some miracle, you make it to your bed, where, to help you fall asleep, you decide between putting on an old episode of *The Office* or playing that podcast you started listening to about Revenge Bedtime Procrastination. *The Office* seems more relaxing. You set your sleep tracker, all seven of your alarms and have one last scroll of everything to make sure the world will still be there when you wake up. You can't wait to go to sleep because you read online that iPhones don't appear in dreams, and a break sounds nice. Fun, even.

Instead of a break, you're visited by the Victorian child. They tell you that you've wasted your evening because you never found out if the MILF fell in love, you didn't send the work emails, the world will be no different after you shared that infographic and you didn't go to the gym. You show them all the cool videos you sent to your friends.

They call you a hypocrite for complaining all day about being tracked and surveilled by whoever 'Big Tech' is, while you've opted in for your sleep, heart rate, productivity, music-listening habits and friend counts to be traced 24/7. You show them your extremely impressive Spotify Wrapped.

They point out that you bought all these screens to distract you from real life, but they've actually made you more aware and anxious about real life than ever. You show them the meditation app you use to balance it all out.

The next evening as you go to sink into your couch, you feel the nagging of the Victorian child who has now become your conscience. For a brief moment, you wish you could shove an iPad into their hands so they'll leave you alone. But instead, you pick up a book, because they might've had a point.

Is nothing sacred anymore?
By Lucy

Has anything good ever come from a work Christmas party? The year is 2022, and everyone's still adjusting to a maskless existence and remembering what joy is again. What better way to celebrate than to reunite the random office band Bel and I had helped form for a wedding-reception-energied gig in a bowls club run by old men who've never seen women carrying things before? One of us is setting up the drums, the other about to do a mic test, and we're trying to win over one of the aforementioned old men so he'll let us ramp up the volume.

'Any requests?' we yell.

'I prefer blondes, I think.'

The band has had a total of three rehearsals and we decide at the last minute to include a cover of New Zealand's unofficial national anthem, 'Royals' by Lorde. It's not good, but it doesn't have to be – this is just for us.

Until something terrible happens.

LUCY: bel
BEL
ur not gonna believe this but someone took a video of that performance and sent it to her
this town is too small

					BEL: To who? Lorde?
					Noooooo
		That performance was never meant to leave those four walls
		Why do I feel like someone's dredged up footage from my
					high school talent quest

LUCY: I KNOW
she was probably like
why are these teenage girls murdering my song

					BEL: Or do you think it was uplifting
					Like
		Wow the cultural cut through I must have in my hometown

LUCE: no I think it would have been more like
hun u got the notes all wrong or
why are you trying so hard to be famous

					BEL: I hope I never see that video again
					I hope no one sees that video again

LUCY: this just in: she gave it a simple exclamation point
react

					BEL: I die a thousand deaths
					Hard out here
					Be a woman

>   Have hobbies
>   Jesus heck

LUCY: guess i'm never getting to interview her again

CHAPTER 8

Ugh, let me live

Good revenge, chic solitude and chasing down joy.

Give me a life I want to close my phone to get back to
By Lucy and Bel

What's worth really caring about?

We're so easily led to think that when we reach a certain milestone there'll be a magic moment when we finally 'love ourselves' and 'get' the world. Our lives will reach a perfect equilibrium and everything will finally make sense. We'll stop dating people who take 72 hours to text back, find friends who fill the space perfectly, subvert the power structures that have kept our freedoms at bay and finally make enough money to be calm enough to post about being grateful for the small things.

This is just not how it works.

Life is a living, breathing thing: it's in motion and it's imperfect. Getting comfortable with the very idea of this is the key to unlocking the chaos both of the world and in our own heads. It's not the answer. But it is the beginning. From there, it becomes about finding a hopeful belief in a future that we can't quite imagine or may not even exist yet. Like our jobs. Like the people we might meet. The places we could go. The events or what might transpire if we open up to the world enough so it can make itself available in return.

And so, it works like this:

You will change. The world will get hotter, and wetter, and smaller, and bigger, and more disappointing, and more boring, and more ALIVE. To judge yourself on past decisions is to miss the point, which is to wake up every day as curious as possible and as forgiving as you can without relinquishing your self-respect. Accept that bad times are inevitable, but with them come times that are the total opposite.

Being OK with yourself in real life is one of the biggest acts of rebellion against everyone who profits off you when you're not. We have to figure out how to live with this feeling without terrorising ourselves or others. And we have to care about the world around us, just not at the expense of our own wellbeing. What follows are our notes for doing just that.

Cringe to think the answers are already in you?
By Lucy

Everyone's always telling us to 'trust our gut' as if we're born with this organ that holds the wisdom of an old owl or a philosopher or something. If that were the case, and we all possessed this all-knowing Magic 8 ball, then we wouldn't have divorce, mid-life crises or Sylvia Plath's fig tree metaphor.

Fridge magnets and vitamin ads are constantly reminding us that we only get one life. The tricky part is knowing what the hell to do with it. You finish school and wonder if you should go to university or travel or become a day trader or get into knitting or have kids or, hell, what if you just did it all? All the people online seem to. Remember when watching a movie didn't require hours of flicking between streaming services, scrolling through every title that's ever existed and retiring before you've found one because, actually, it's time for bed now? Don't get me wrong, I love the internet, but it really has supercharged the number of decisions we have to make daily, diluting our gut instincts with every new display of whatever seems hotter, better, faster or more fun that day. No wonder none of us can get a clear reading on how the hell we actually feel about things.

There's that iconic part in *Fleabag* where she sits in the confession booth and admits how much she just wants someone to decide all the big and small things in life for her: what to wear, eat, listen to, who to love and who to trust. She's like, I'm so tired! Someone tell me what to DO! Annoyingly, with the absence of a hot priest and a finely tuned script to move our lives along, we have to learn how not to argue with ourselves and listen to our own instincts. Something tells me we've all become a bit deprogrammed from listening to them, in case they turn out wrong, and we have no one to blame but ourselves. It sucks having to be responsible for your own life, I get it.

We can outsource this guidance to Pinterest boards and 'how I got here' videos, but the antidote to decision-making hell is trusting your gut and strengthening it as if it were any other muscle.

Put me on a panel in a pink sock and a sneaker, and I would tell you this:

- Have a period of time where being alone is your default. It's hard to listen to your instincts when there's always someone talking over them.
- Let go of the idea that intuition comes to you in the way you see in the movies. Your path won't come to you in a premonition, a dream, inside a fortune cookie or on the tarot card that you scrolled past last night that told you to 'stop what you're doing and listen! If you're seeing this, it was meant for you!'
- Stop seeing envy as an ugly emotion and, instead, let it show you what you want or what you're missing.
- Open the email and remember your initial reaction to it.

- Take the meeting, but listen to the little nagging feeling telling you that the person on the other end doesn't see your vision.
- Take the next one and feel the rush of relief telling you that this person does.
- Turn relief into your favourite emotion. Make it the arrow you follow. Remember that it's always there, on the other side of discomfort and uncertainty, and chase it down.
- When you meet someone new, investigate whether you like the way they make you feel or if you just want some company. Either is okay, but only one scenario deserves a second coffee.
- Learn to tell the difference between intuition and impulse. Like when you're in the middle of one of the lectures you're spending tens of thousands of dollars on, and the thought, 'Hmm, I could just leave' barges in. That's not your intuition – that's being at university. Or, when you're four wines deep, and you think now would be a good time to make out with the person you've been friends with for years but who you definitely don't really want to kiss. Yes, you have a feeling in your gut. No, it's not intuition: it's wine.
- Understand that knowing what you don't want is just as useful as knowing what you do.
- Lastly, and most importantly, make your decisions and give yourself permission to enjoy them.
- Because once you figure it out, doing what you want feels so good.

A woman alone is an exotic thing
By Lucy and Bel

It's so easy to be fooled into believing that solitude is a failure. Living part of our lives online (in whatever capacity you play, work or socialise on it) convinces us that everyone else is out at some birthday brunch in a designer outfit having a good time while we're stuck alone finding a damp sock left in the washing machine. Obviously, this is a lie, but it gets exhausting to be constantly confronted with the idea that everyone has someone but you.

Here are the scenes we don't often see:

- Waking up in your bed, unable to move on a Monday morning from the weight of having to handle it all on your own.
- Being emo in grey marl, socks and slides on a weeknight, buying something from the supermarket to cook dinner, which you're going to have to eat for the next five meals.
- Going to weddings and being forced upon a straggler in the bridal party after being spotlit as single.
- Buying medicine in the pharmacy in your pyjamas when you're sick.
- Wrestling your own luggage at the airport.

- Eating Burger King in a food court alone.
- The sound of the refrigerator in your apartment ticking over again . . .

These tiny, mundane things can crush you if they pile on top of each other while you're in a lonely phase. We can sink and be swallowed whole or decide something altogether braver: that solitude is a chance for us to become more knowable to ourselves and more available to life. At its worst, the loneliness of your own company can make you feel like you'd literally pay someone to come around and spoon you on the sofa just to feel physical contact. At its best, we can see it as a chance for some self-indulgence, to go and get lost for a little while in our own lives and not have to consider anybody else's urges in the context of our own.

Yes, I'm alone at the bar, and no, I haven't been stood up

Getting good at being alone has been made particularly difficult for women, as though it's exotic if we happen to be by ourselves, choose to be solo or are content in our own company. This seems to manifest, strangely, at its peak in restaurants. Perhaps it gives onlookers the threatening feeling that feasting on our own lives is enough? A table where you're trying to turn the pages of a book with one hand while eating a fork of pasta with the other can be one of the loneliest places alive. Or it can lift the top off to new ways of feeling and knowing how to be comfortable with ourselves.

Remedying the initial discomfort of being a woman alone can start here, in this very restaurant. You can whip out your notebook, whether you consider yourself a 'writer' or not, or periodically look up and smile to assure everyone that you chose to be here and you're not waiting on anyone. You can leave your friend a seven-minute voice note, drink a lot of alcohol or take Jemima Kirke's advice and maybe just stop thinking about yourself so much. When you master this, you'll find yourself watching a group of people take photos of their food and each other and be glad you are far away from the debate about what image to make the cover of their photo dump ('It has to look like I'm not trying, but do you think the microgreens pop enough?').

Loneliness looks chic when Sofia Coppola films it, feels bleak when we're drowning in it

You'd think that the biggest risk of getting too good at being alone is that you'd go for a walk, fall off a cliff and hope that you had a plan with a friend that afternoon so that when you don't turn up, someone actually notices. The more likely scenario is that you get so good at being on your own, only having to worry about your own needs, running on your own time and being able to say and do what is best for you that you stop letting others in.

For some of us, being alone can feel socially safe – addictive even. Maybe this started in the school parking lot when your parents were late to pick you up, so you started planning how you were going to raise yourself from now on. Or in the grocery line when your mum ran off to grab that thing she'd forgotten, and as you inched closer to the cashier, you frantically tried to think of a repayment plan for all the items that had already been scanned. In these moments, where you felt like you were all on your own and you were unprepared, you never wanted that feeling again. So you decided to build a life where you don't have to rely on anyone else.

Not having FOMO is fine when you really don't want to go to that three-day festival with less than satisfactory washing facilities and shit headliners, but bad when you're figuring out ways to leave your best friend's party before you've even arrived. Letting yourself want and be wanted is a fact of life, and getting too good at being alone can get in the way of that. Remember that you owe a little bit of your goodness to others.

Just be cute for you

Don't let being alone make you give up on the magic of the world. We've been taught that solitude is intrinsically linked with despair and that when you're in the depths, it'll go on forever. It's like, why go to the party if you're going to stand in the kitchen and feel like you're watching the movies of others' lives? Why take the trip if it's just going to be you in your same body, but somewhere else? Why leave the house when you'll be surrounded by people who are successful and happy enough to know what to do with their lives? On and on these dark thoughts can go, hanging around your neck, collecting each other like heavy beads along the way as a reminder that no one cares whether or not you're getting to bed on time or eating the whole food pyramid.

But what if, instead, we thought of loneliness like this?

1) A natural experience of being alive that, no matter how much love or light you have in your life, will leave eventually in the same way it came.

2) A sign that there's an absence of joy, so here's a chance to go and find a new way to feel it.

The second part demands energy that's hard to channel if you're feeling at the end of the world: being brave. The second part is a chance to go and chase down something new and find out what fills you up outside of what you've seen online or what you've been led to believe you should want. The second part is the home you'll spend your whole life returning to.

Ad campaign ideas to help 21st-century women feel better about the world
By Bel

MOTION IS EMOTION: A gym where you type in your feelings onto an iPad at the entrance each time you go, and they customise your workout accordingly.

THIS IS NOT A CALL TO ARMS. IT'S A MANIFESTO FOR LIFE: A life insurance policy for women that pays your next of kin all the money you missed out on because of the gender pay gap.

TO BE IS TO FEEL: A campaign for a completely unrelated appliance, like a toasted sandwich maker or a waffle machine, that has somehow linked pressing bread together with feminine fragility. Comes in lemon yellow as a progressive colourway option.

SHEOS: A new brand of ergonomic high heels designed for women in the workplace that also prevents shin splints.

I WORK, THEREFORE I AM: Scientifically proven skincare that both works and connects you with a career mentor when you spend over $499 on your first purchase.

Come and get it

Joy is the tonic to every single ache in your body and every thread of lies online.
Joy is resistance.
Joy is touching things and feeling them on the inside.
Joy is running down the hot road laughing, not having to think about the future.
Joy is a sign things are going right – tap into it in your body.
Joy is crushing on someone who might just change your life.
Joy is doing nothing and not feeling bad about it.
Joy is worry lifting without you noticing.
Joy is coming for you, and you need to be ready for it.
Joy is so good you can't touch it.
Joy is everything changing just when you thought it was over.
Joy is a work day passing fast.
Joy is not Cate Blanchett's character after a divorce.
Joy is the perfect temperature.
Joy is not exclusively reserved for rich people on boats or people with clean hair.
Joy exists in the mundane slivers of life just as much as its supercuts. Joy sometimes needs to be hunted down, which seems hard and tiring when there's all this work to do.
Joy is sometimes the only thing we've got.

Joy is both wanting the same thing.
Joy is the windows open at night.
Joy is pulling the clutch out and refusing to feel bad about it.
Joy is welcoming good danger.
Joy is dancing – not *Step Up 2: The Streets* style (enviable) but just moving, hovering above reality and not thinking about what you look like for as long as humanly possible.
Joy is not a foreign language.
Joy is not an endless season.
Joy is not to be messed with – come and get it.

Yeah, the internet is great, but have you tried
By Lucy

- Waking up naturally before your alarm.
- Even better, waking up and realising you have a few more hours to sleep in.
- Having the exact change you need for that thing you bought.
- When none of the necklaces you packed for the trip got tangled in your bag.
- And your headphones didn't either.
- Finding a matching set of dishes in a thrift store.
- Getting a parking space that you can drive right through so you don't need to reverse out.
- Finding a heart-shaped rock.
- When someone cancels a meeting you were dreading.
- Finishing the whole cup of coffee before it gets lukewarm.
- Filling a measuring cup perfectly on your first try.
- Stopping the microwave exactly as the timer goes off.
- A perfectly ripe avocado.
- When you switch radio stations, and they're both playing the same song.
- Finishing both your shampoo and conditioner at the same time.

- Hitting three green lights in a row.
- Switching back to your TV show right as the ads finish.
- Hitting that perfect high-five.
- When your leftovers perfectly fit in the container.
- A song finishing just as you arrive at your destination.
- Grabbing the exact number of hangers for the clothes you need to hang up.
- A surprise discount on the thing you were going to buy anyway.
- Finishing a chapter precisely when you want to fall asleep.
- Finding the butterfly that fell off the back of your earring.
- Coming home from a night out with your keys, wallet and an unsmashed phone.

Rewenge is anything good happening to you at any given time
By Bel

Rewenge (pronounced: re-wen-gay) means treating everything good that happens to you as your own personal revenge. Rewenge is sweeter than revenge, because it can be any tiny good thing that happens to you: karmic reward for any time you've ever been wronged. The concept is inspired by a catchphrase used in an episode of *Peep Show*. We've appropriated it here, and are now gifting it to you to use as much as you require. You're welcome.

Rewenge is your reward for continuing to live and believing you might just win again one day.
Rewenge is the small triumphs that could be missed by the untrained eye or if you're not properly watching out for them.
Rewenge is admitting some people are better than others, that you are one of them and that any good thing that happens to you is what you deserve.
Rewenge is gratitude for the small things but not in a yoga-studio-inspirational-quote kind of way, more like a sharp acknowledgement that life is on your side.

Not tired this morning?
Rewenge.
The wheels of the plane lifting up to a new life?
Rewenge.
Seeing a former tryst looking tired coming out of a convenience store?
Rewenge.
Good weather on the holiday?
Rewenge.
Happy hour? Rewenge. Keys at the top of your bag?
Rewenge.
Home before sunset?
Rewenge.
A date that doesn't feel like you're screaming in your mind?
Rewenge.
Fast day at work?
Rewenge.
Not having to think about what to make for dinner?
Rewenge.
Money left over after payday?
Rewenge.
Ordering a pair of shoes online that fit?
Rewenge.
Socks come, too?
Rewenge.
Getting a car parking spot exactly where you need it?
Rewenge.
Literally just having a good day?
Rewenge.
Promotion? Rewenge. Falling in love with someone great?

Rewenge.
Muting someone online?
Rewenge.
Catching the bus when you were about to miss it?
Rewenge.
When the orchid flowers after a year of being a stick?
Rewenge.
A table free by the window? Rewenge. Good hair?
Rewenge.
The exact thing you were after?
Rewenge.

The tiniest thing in life being good, whether you expected it or not? Rewenge for anyone or anything that's ever wronged you and a sign this will continue to happen if you know how to look out for it.

How not to ruin your own life

Don't make me feel bad for my feelings.
Don't make me feel like this job is the only thing I've got.
Don't wear me down so much I don't want to get out of bed.
Don't make me feel special if you don't believe it.
Don't pretend like we've had the same amount of luck.
Don't make out like not everything's political.
Don't pretend you're not also figuring it out as you go along.
Don't make this all about you.
Don't forget my name on purpose. Don't forget me.
Don't ask me when I'm going to have children.
Don't stand by and watch me rob myself of joy.
Don't make me believe this was all for nothing.
Don't let me waste my money on shit that isn't worth it.
Don't let this not be worth it.
Don't make this feel like it's not the real thing.
Don't let me waste this life on someone else's vision.
Don't let me be lonely in this city.
Don't not tell me what you want and get mad at me for not knowing.
Don't be elusive when you could be transparent.
Don't think the answers will all come at once – who are you, God?
Don't be afraid of saying no; what's the worst that could happen?

Don't text back for a while, and see how you feel.
Don't think all these feelings are forever.
Don't question anything good when it comes along.
Don't be afraid of wanting more, you deserve it.

Out here trying to feel self-love because my cleanser told me to
By Bel

Malaysia, 2022

On the scooter riding back from the beach through dappled light, Lisa's hands are around my waist, our clothes damp and dirty from the heat. I drive slowly so that we can talk.

We're talking about whether we love ourselves more or less than we did when we met 12 years ago, when we were doing PR for technology brands and buying ad space for companies who didn't really need it. Are we better women now? Do we finally love who we are? What is self-love anyway? We use the term almost sarcastically, because it's been co-opted by so many banks and skincare brands that it's hard to know whether it's even real.

'Self-love is loving my body,' I say.

'Self-love is loving my personality,' she says.

'Self-love is not being jealous of things I'll never have.'

'Self-love is going vegan for the planet, but sometimes eating meat because of my iron deficiency.'

'Self-love is spending the dregs of my pay cheque on a manicure.'

'Self-love is loving my tits and not hating my arms.'

'Self-love is not replying to everyone all the time.'

'Self-love is stopping being so nice in emails.'

'Self-love is taking myself to the movies and not feeling like a freak.'

'Self-love is writing in my journal as if I could lead a cacao ceremony with complete conviction.'

'Self-love is not hating myself for sometimes hating life.'

'Self-love is in the company I choose to keep.'

'Self-love is . . . ME.'

What is modern self-love? It's waking up every day and forgiving yourself for not being someone else's vision of perfection and instead being your own. It's, as bell hooks describes, giving your own self the love you're dreaming of. It's refusing to believe you are one purchase or curated post away from arriving at a paradise that others are already living in.

I accelerate so we can make it up the hill. We yell the lyrics of Yusef Stephen's 'Wild World' into the wind. On the other side of trying to do everything so flawlessly lies what we all really want: freedom.

Modern Euphoria

The meeting being cancelled. Annual leave: no emails, please. The sensation of sun on your skin, but not in a burning UV-warning way, just a healthy glow, like a Garnier BB cream. Two clean socks slipping into two clean shoes. Hearing back from your crush within a short timeframe. Forgetting to check your phone and nothing bad happening. Waking up and wanting to get up. Getting up and wanting to be up. Knowing where you're going without using Google Maps. Having enough time to get there. Dramatic WhatsApp voice notes that could either be the plot of an award-winning TV show or just you and your friends' lives. Good drama. Nice hair. Feeling happy, but not like you have to post about it. Leaving your laptop at the office. Getting paid and somehow having some left over. A soft breeze on the way home. Carrying one half-empty tote bag and having everything you need. Pulling the clutch out. Saying no and staying in. Clean sheets. Getting through another week. Outfits not for photographing, just for living in. Memories in your phone that remind you of who you once were and how far you've come.

Best-case scenario: Good Hair
By Bel

If I were granted three wishes, obviously, the first two would be world peace and gender equality, but the third would be to have good hair. It feels right and fair that one of them could be something completely self-indulgent and basic after being so selfless with the other two, and I would do anything never to have to wake up again wanting to completely renovate my head like I can a Sims character's.

People with good hair don't get it. They have the kind of conviction of private school boys or people who genuinely enjoy running and consider it a good use of their time. They don't know what it's like out here, in reality.

You'll truly come to know how lucky good-hair people are when one day all yours is cut off without your consent. I'd gone to see a new hairdresser on my lunch break because mine – the famous Nadia, who all my friends went to – got carpal tunnel syndrome and ruined our lives by having to switch to colouring. I schlepped to a different salon near my work and made the mistake of being on my phone the whole time, only to glance up and find I resembled a hedgehog.

There's a lesson here. And the lesson is, if you cheat on a good hairdresser, you will always pay. If you want a dramatic transformation, you'll always be dramatically surprised. Go to yoga. Go to a psychic. Buy a hat. But be careful who you trust with a pair of scissors and a photo of someone slightly hotter than you that you found on the internet.

This is where my friend comes in. I can't tell you her full name. Otherwise, everyone will track her down and get the number of her hairdresser, and there will be no appointments left for those of us who need good hair the most.

One afternoon, she came to my house after taking a Xanax. She'd ended a long-term relationship: she went away for a weekend, met someone else, came back and ended it. We're sitting in the brick courtyard out the back of my flat as she tells me the story.

'Incredible,' I say. It's the end of spring, and a horny warm wind runs in the air.

'Honestly? I feel incredible. Afterwards, I went to the hairdresser, got this done, and now I feel like I look like a Russian spy.'

'You do,' I reply. She does. She looks like one of the characters Lucy Liu dresses up as in *Charlie's Angels*. I'm jealous. It's amazing what you can accomplish after a breakup. Snip snip, my friends and I say to describe any major decision we've made to get rid of something terrible. Maybe I could date someone just to break up with them and go to the hairdresser and get the same look.

It's 4pm on a Tuesday and I'm meant to be working from home, but there's always another time to work when you have a Russian spy for a friend, a bottle of house white in the fridge and a dramatic circumstance unfolding in front of your eyes. I want to know which product she's been told to use so I can be invigorated like her. I want to get rid of my thin, lifeless hair and be one of those women at the helm of her own life, snipping away at whatever's not working.

'I actually don't care about anything,' she breathes. We're smoking by this stage. Spy behaviour. I'm absorbing her electricity. 'It's the most freeing feeling.' I'm pretty sure that's what she's saying; I'm busy being jealous of her hair in the light, wondering if going blonde could be the answer to all my troubles. Stylish people have good hair and they have fewer problems. Or maybe they're just better at hiding them because their hair's doing all the work.

In these moments, it's very difficult to say the right thing. You can't say, 'Don't worry, it will be OK,' because that's a promise you can't make. You just have to sit there, trying to keep up until they get up to leave, agreeing to help look after some things and get rid of others and make sure they tell you the name of the hairdresser they went to before they leave.

I've tried to be philosophical about bad haircuts and use them as metaphors for bad things needing time to change. For self-improvement. ('Maybe by the time this is fixed, I'll be fluent in Portuguese! In love! Hotter! Fitter! Happier! Free!') For what we can't control. Or as a reminder of all the significantly larger atrocities in the world beyond my own vanity. Once I went to hear the photographer Marti Friedlander speak. After an hour talking at length about what it was like capturing other people's lives, someone in the audience asked if doing that for so long had affected her own vanity. She replied, 'I don't care if I'm having a bad hair day: that's your problem. I'm not the one who has to look at me.'

But the thing is, when everything else is terrible and uncontrollable, it just feels like good hair is the least you could ask for. It's a shortcut to self-esteem. A therapist would say, 'Let's go deeper on this,' and I would say, 'I want my hair to do what I cannot: be brilliant all the time. Reliable. Shine! End abruptly and not cling onto anything not worth holding onto. Look effortless without trying. Not get caught in life's wind, yet suit its surroundings. Sit in a chic, content way without getting distracted by everyone else. If my hair is right, obviously, so is everything else.'

At the end of what felt like a thousand years (eight months) after the hedgehog incident, I find myself in a new city with split ends, having to trust a stranger all over again. I separate my mind from body and sit down in the chair.

'What are we going for today?' the hairdresser asks.

'I want to look like a Russian spy,' I say. He gets to work.

Unsolicited rules to live by

Treat friendships with the same amount of energy as romantic relationships. Freedom is the best feeling you can chase, and not everyone gets that luxury. Resolution can only come from yourself. Generosity will change your life. Give a lot, but then keep some back just for you. Joy is the best tonic for terror. Chase it down. Refuse to rob yourself of it. Not everyone will love you; get over it. Life is boring sometimes; don't feel bad about it. Giving up nothing is giving up everything. Evacuate your life regularly so you can see things more clearly. Nothing major: taking a new road will do. Go far away, come back and notice the shift. Sometimes everything, sometimes nothing. The faster you accept everyone's a mess, the quicker you can just get on with it. If you're hurt, go straight to the source of pain. Pursuing perfection will ruin your life; try aiming for a B+ every once in a while instead. Constant optimisation robs life of its magic. When you want to pour petrol on your life, pour energy into it instead. If you're depleted, think about what you're giving too much of your energy to and stop. Don't post lies for attention. Keep your real life more interesting than your online one. Keep secrets. Foster mystery. Look after yourself the way you look after someone you love. Don't blame yourself for past mistakes. Let people go away and make their own lives without resistance. Don't feel bad about feeling bad, but change something and stop complaining. Take breaks, or else you will snap in half. The latter is hard to ask for time off for. Running away is fun but will only fix things temporarily. Success can be great but lonely; make sure you share it. Submitting to the process frees you of it. Who cares if it doesn't work out? Take a chance; there's everything to lose. Regret nothing except not doing anything. Stop being afraid of being vulnerable; everyone else is human, too. Ask for help when you need it and offer it in return. You've come this far; don't you even think of giving up. Good luck, and you have everything you need already inside you <3.

EPILOGUE

Tell me what I need to hear, which is that everything's going to be ok
By Bel

International departure lounge, Humberto Delgado Airport, Lisbon, Portugal 2023

Luce comes back from the bar carrying two mini bottles of wine and two glasses, and we sit down at a carefully selected table with a direct view of the boarding details updating on the screen. We're there an hour before check in because we're anxious and because we don't want this to actually be happening.

'Can you believe I had a breakdown in the middle of what was meant to be one of the best times of my life?' Luce laughs. I start laughing, too. We can't stop. The table is shaking. The people seated beside us are giving us confused looks. I've never met anyone who can make the terrible so entertaining.

'You're going to hate what I'm about to say,' I reply, 'It's, like, some internet therapy quote someone from high school would post on their stories.'

'Oh God, well, if not now, then when?' Luce replies. We have a game we often play to pass the time, which we call 'Everything's the same, but . . .'. We go one-for-one, casting stupid visions of ourselves with annoying flaws, like, 'Everything's the same, but . . . I ask you to take heaps of videos of me walking out of the ocean for my Instagram,' or 'Everything's the same, but . . . I just cannot, for the life of me, figure out where Europe is even though we're living in it.' It's funny that this comes to my mind as we're sitting here, Luce with all her life packed up in front of us, about to fly back to New Zealand. I take a deep breath. 'What if everything's perfect?' I start. 'What if you had to come here, to feel all these things, to try and fail and see it all for yourself to know it's what you didn't want?'

Luce tops up her glass. 'I know what you're trying to say, but right now, I cannot fathom anything being perfect. This does feel like a scene in a movie, though.'

'Life's a movie.'

'Yeah, one where I have to tell everyone I've failed. How fucking embarrassing.'

'Or you can just tell them that you tried?' I take a sip. 'Or we could lie.' Another flight's details flip over on the board. 'Or . . . or we could use our comms degrees and formulate a PR response that avoids all the truthful answers altogether?'

Luce says nothing for a while, and I know this is of the most frustrating scenarios to be in: sitting somewhere feeling like your life's burned down, and the person opposite trying to tell you it'll all be OK and using dumb jokes to prove it.

'No, Bel, why does this feel like the philosophical scene in *Mamma Mia*?!'

'You know I fucking love ABBA.'

'You know I love a white wine spritzer at an airport.'

'I'm going to sound like a parent now, but I'm very proud of you and I promise you'll phoenix out of this.'

'I can't wait for that feeling.'

'It'll come.'

'Not now.'

'Not now, but soon.'

'I guess everything's just for now anyway.'

The details of Luce's flight are the next to click over on the board. We throw back the last of our wine and heave the baggage trolley towards the counter, the weight of it making us manoeuvre wildly across the lino floor. For such a heavy moment, it feels light and fun, as though the adventure is just beginning, not coming to a crashing halt. The second we join the queue, both our phones chime with an email carrying the latest round of book cover designs to review.

'Isn't this so us?' Luce laughs. 'Working 'til the minute I get on a flight halfway around the world?'

'I wouldn't have it any other way.'

'If only everyone knew how much goes on behind the scenes.'

'If only everyone knew what we've got to get through,' I say, selfishly now thinking about what lies ahead: writing this book.

'Bel, if anyone can do this, you can,' she says. Friends have a way of seeing things about ourselves that we never can in these fragile moments.

'I'm thinking the exact same thing about you.'

We hug goodbye, Luce disappears into customs, and the dream – a dream – is over. I take an Uber back to our half-empty apartment, the peak hour traffic so bad I swear by the time I get home, Luce would have already taken flight. The keys hitting the kitchen bench make an 'alone again' sound, and I think about the days and months to come: squashing my life into another set of suitcases, trawling the internet to make more plans, fighting for a place to sleep in another housing crisis, making work work, saving enough money, finding friends. All the same things lie waiting for her on the other side of the 32-hour journey home. I know we're both afraid.

We pack up. We lift off. We land. We face reality. We start again. Things get good. We get complacent. Then they get hard. We work them out. Then they get good again. You can never be too established to restart your own life and put it back together in a way you never thought possible. I've met people in almost every decade of their life who've reaffirmed this to me over and over again. The thing is, there are all these uncontrollable things that will happen to us that, in the moment, feel like the worst thing in the world. Lucy and I even laugh that we will look back over this book in years to come and cringe at our younger selves, for thinking our feelings about certain things were that important, or that minor events seemed like major harrowing chapters when they were happening.

It's hopeful feeling we will be able to make sense of these experiences in hindsight but can never fully predict when they'll come and change us for the good. There must be a word for that.

> **LUCY:** i just found the letter you slipped in my bag
> which i can't open
> because i'll start crying
> and i won't stop
> BEL
> UGH idk what's going to happen to me

BEL: Things will feel very hard for a while
Then they'll slowly get good
And I'll be here whenever that happens
And I'll know it's happened because you'll message me and say
BEL I feel alive and excited about what's possible
And you'll lift off all over again
xx

ACKNOWLEDGEMENTS

This book was inspired by the truest of friendships, the deepest of obsessions and our own personal God: the internet.

Thank you to the millions of people who give us regular, electric validation on the internet. You helped us take our online ideas into the physical realm, and believe they were worth writing down in the first place.

To our agent, Abigail Bergstrom, for taking a chance on two women from the corner of the world, and our editor, Jane Sturrock, for working our chaos into existence.

To the wider Quercus/Hachette team and everyone else involved in the inspiration, writing, publication and marketing of this book, we wouldn't be here without you.

To everyone who had to put up with us as we mined you for experiences and tested new phrases on you to see if they landed: you know who you are and we are so grateful.

And lastly, thank you to everyone who underestimated us. You helped us find the gumption to do this. x

Shit You Should Care About was launched as a WordPress blog by three best friends in the back of a political science lecture. Today, it's a global ecosystem of content: two podcasts, 3.4 million Instagram followers and a daily newsletter.

Lucy Blakiston launched Shit You Should Care About with her two best friends, aged 21, and within a year the platform had become a global success, with millions of followers. The voice and CEO of SYSCA, Lucy is the editorial director of the company and frequently speaks and advises on how to connect with Gen Z on an international stage.

Bel Hawkins is a published poet, writer and beloved SYSCA contributor. She's won leading awards in advertising and media and spent the majority of her 20s living around the world, working on projects that speak directly to worn-out women, helping people phoenix and making them feel less alone in the world.

shityoushouldcareabout.com
ShitYouShouldCareAbout